BUSINESS LETTERS FOR ARTISTS

 M. STEPHEN DOHERTY

WATSON-GUPTILL PUBLICATIONS · NEW YORK

ACKNOWLEDGMENTS

I would like to thank Mary Suffudy and Candace Raney for suggesting the idea for this book and challenging me to write it; Dale Ramsey for editing my words into a consistent and accurate text; and Robert Fillie for his excellent design of the publication. I am also indebted to several artists, agents, and attorneys who reviewed drafts of the text, including John Howard Sanden, Marian MacKinney, Harley Bartlett, Stella Golden, Francis X. Morrissey, and Frank Feldman. My deepest thanks go to my wife, Sara, for her abiding love and support.

Edited by Dale Ramsey
Designed by Robert Fillie
Graphic production by Hector Campbell

Published by Watson-Guptill Publications,
a division of BPI Communications, Inc.,
1515 Broadway, New York, NY 10036

Cataloging-in Publication data are available through the Library of Congress, Washington,DC.

Printed in Mexico
First printing, 1993

1 2 3 4 5 / 97 96 95 94 93

Contents

Introduction

This book is for the artist who finds it awkward, if not unpleasant, to draw up a legal contract that defines, in great detail, his or her business relationship with a collector, gallery owner, publisher, or portrait client. The fifteen letters in this book can have all the force of formal contracts, yet they are written in a language that is more appropriate for the kinds of friendly agreements artists establish. Instead of referring to people as "parties" and starting each sentence with the word "whereas," these letters ask the recipients to acknowledge what has been discussed (or should be discussed) in normal conversation.

But, you may ask, how can a one-page friendly letter offer the same legal protection as a five-page contract? The answer is that it can't—but it doesn't have to.

In all likelihood, that five-page contract would scare away the gallery owner, portrait agent, or collector with whom you want to do business. All you need in most business situations is a letter that establishes your basic rights, privileges, and responsibilities. A friendly letter therefore becomes the best way—if not the only way—of guaranteeing your basic rights.

Make no mistake: if properly administered, these fifteen letters are, in fact, legal contracts. A legal contract is simply an agreement between two or more parties that is legally enforceable. To have such an agreement requires a meeting of minds on the essential terms of the arrangement. Although some *oral* agreements are enforceable, there is no doubt that a *written* agreement is preferable. In oral agreements, memories fade or disappear, and opportunities to distort or deny increase. Furthermore, though it is better to have the signature of each party on a written agreement, it is not always necessary. Courts will enforce the terms of a letter setting forth one party's understanding of an agreement if it is reasonable to assume that the other party has had an opportunity to object and if the parties acted as set forth in the letter.

As the first paragraph of each letter states, the letter reviews discussions that have been conducted in person, in previous correspondence, or over the phone. Thus, the best way to use one of the letters is to read it and make notes of the items it covers before you call on the person with whom you want to do business. Next, you telephone or visit that person so you can discuss each of the items. As each question is discussed and resolved, make notes about what was decided. Back at your studio or office, write the person a letter using this book and your notes as a guide.

In the following pages, preceding the actual letters, each letter is analyzed, paragraph by paragraph, so you can better understand the intention. There are also suggestions for modifying the paragraphs to meet your particular needs, as well as cautions about words that will be important in establishing your rights and privileges. If, in adapting the letters, you are uncomfortable with certain adjectives or phrases (such as "I would be delighted," and so on), substitute them with words from your own vocabulary. Just take care not to add phrases like "if you want to," or "if it's alright with you," which would build a loophole into the letter through which the recipient can easily escape.

Note that at the bottom of each letter, the person to whom it is addressed is asked to acknowledge, and thereby certify, his or her agreement. The signatures will complete the contractual agreement. In the event that the other person either neglects or refuses to sign the letter, it is possible to evidence the agreement in other ways. One way is to send a letter along with the artwork that person will be exhibiting, publishing, or buying, stating that by accepting the artwork he or she is agreeing to the terms established in your original correspondence.

The letters you send, and the signed copies you receive, should become part of a file you maintain. That file should contain all your receipts, insurance forms, exhibit announcements, and letters related to the individual, gallery, or corporation you are doing business with. In the event that you need to pursue a claim against (let us say) a gallery, any and all of that file could become useful in proving that the agreements were established and that subsequent actions were taken.

While these letters should be very useful in conducting business in the art world, there will be times when they are inadequate for covering all the issues related to a business proposition. In situations where you have a long list of requests, conditions, exclusions, or limitations to detail in a contract, you should hire a lawyer who can write and/or negotiate that contract for you.

As you work with people in the art world, keep in mind that ethical considerations may become as important as legal considerations in your career. For example, you may wind up in a situation where you know you have the legal *right* to do something, but you also recognize that such an action might be considered unethical, unfair, or unreasonable by your peers. As one lawyer pointed out when reviewing the text of this book, "good ethics and morals generally lead to good business."

You should also understand that having a signed letter of agreement or a lengthy contract will not guarantee that you will be able to receive payments that are due or win a lawsuit against the person who has violated the agreement. It is extremely difficult and costly to sue someone for an unpaid bill, particularly when the amount is not large or the defendant lives outside the jurisdiction of the law courts where you live. The contracts and supporting documents in your files will be extremely helpful in proving your side of the argument, but the ultimate decision will be in the hands of a judge or jury. When you believe that your rights have been violated, your best recourse is to consult a lawyer about what course of action to take.

As you work with these letters, you'll see that certain legal issues come up repeatedly. The following offers an introduction to those issues.

COPYRIGHT

Copyright is the ownership of the right to reproduce a visual image, written material, or a piece of music. Who owns the copyright may depend on when the work was created and who may have published or performed the material, but, generally speaking, the presumption of the law is now in favor of the artist, writer, or musician. Unless someone can prove you have transferred the copyright to your artwork, it is assumed that you own it.

It is important to understand that the copyright to a piece of artwork does not transfer to the person who buys the physical work. Just because someone buys a painting does not mean that person has the right to reproduce it, alter it, or in any way infringe upon your copyright. The law does not even require you to put a copyright notice (encircled "c") on your painting, print, or sculpture, though it is advisable to do so, for a measure of protection.

A separate issue concerning the copyright to derivative works—prints or reproductions based on original artwork—is addressed with Letter 9.

CONSIGNMENT LAWS

More than 25 states have adopted statutes that protect artists who leave their artwork on consignment with a gallery. These laws offer some protection against having the artwork considered part of the gallery's assets in the event that the gallery does not meet its financial obligations. The statutes provide that the relationship between the artist and dealer is a fiduciary one. That is, it assumes there is a high degree of trust, good faith, and responsibility, as between a trustee and a beneficiary of a trust, and that the artwork delivered by the artist to the dealer constitutes "trust property . . . for the benefit of the consignor" (i.e., the artist). With that assumption, creditors of the gallery cannot obtain these assets.

Unfortunately, reality is not as reassuring as the theory behind the statutes, for some dealers do commingle the cash received from the sale of an artist's work with their own funds, do not keep funds in separate bank accounts, and do not account and remit payments to artists as required. The statutes are not self-executing, meaning that artists must police the operations of galleries themselves.

AGENCY AGREEMENTS

Because gallery owners act as agents for the artists whose artwork they exhibit, the general law of agency is applicable to the relationship. It is important to establish whether the gallery is an exclusive agent for the artist. You'll note that Letters 4, 5, and 11 in this book are designed to clarify the agency agreement.

THE RESPONDING LETTER

It is unlikely that there will be only one piece of correspondence between you and the dealers, publishers, or agents with whom you do business. The person who receives your letter of agreement may respond in a follow-up letter in an attempt to clarify intentions or the relationship. The "clarification" may inadvertently—or may intentionally—insert language into the agreement that will become part of the contractual relationship. You should treat these responding letters as potential revisions or alterations of your original letter.

Beginning a Business Relationship with a Group Exhibition

WHEN TO USE THIS LETTER

The first opportunity artists usually have to exhibit in a gallery occurs when they are invited to submit art-work for a group exhibition. There is often some uni-fying theme to a show—self-portraits, vanitas still lifes, or local landscapes—and the dealer brings together artwork both by the artists he or she repre-sents on a regular basis and those who do not have such representation. The aim is to round out the exhi-bition and gauge collectors' responses to new artists' work.

Because this is likely to be the first occasion on which the artist and dealer work together, this letter has two objectives: First, to provide information that might be helpful in selling the pictures; and, second, to make sure that certain basic expectations are understood and agreed upon.

IMPORTANT POINTS TO CONSIDER

Paragraph ❷

If you can enclose pertinent material with your letter (or if you are rewriting this letter to customize it), don't hesitate to offer specific comments about your paintings or your professional accomplishments. Dealers often find that relating personal anecdotes, pointing to important passages in a painting, or con-necting one painting to another, help to create inter-est in an artist's work. Furthermore, you want this exhibition to lead to others, so help the dealer to know you better.

Paragraphs ❸ and ❹

Most critical among the business expectations to be defined with this letter are the financial ones. All too often, artists and dealers avoid discussing exactly what will happen in the event that a painting sells; the artists then wind up accepting less than they expected, because the dealer has a practice of discounting, extending payments, or paying slowly. What could have been a pleasant and profitable relationship turns sour simply because the artist failed to ask for a set of reasonable financial terms. You should establish the price of each painting, the policy with regard to discounting and extending payments, the dealer percentage, and the schedule for payments. Terms that are fairly standard have been filled in for this sample. If you get a dealer to state his or her policy—whatever it may be—you have a better chance of avoiding problems.

Paragraph ❺

Many dealers are reluctant to give an artist the names and addresses of the individuals or corpora-tions who purchase the artist's work, especially when the dealer has no experience working with that artist. The fear is that the artist will simply bypass the dealer and sell artwork directly to the gallery's clients.

Under these circumstances, you should be willing to strike out Paragraph 5, even though it is written as a request, not a demand. In time, you may be able to win the dealer's confidence in your profes-sionalism; he or she may then divulge the names of those who have purchased your work.

Paragraph ❻

If, in your preliminary discussion, the dealer agrees to pay the cost of picture framing or of shipping to and from the gallery, you should not fail to thank him or her for covering those expenses; but make sure, also, that you establish that there will be insur-ance coverage while the pictures are in transit.

Dealer's Name
Gallery Name
Street Address
City, State, Zip

Dear _____:

I am very pleased to have my artwork included in your upcoming group exhibition from _____ to _____. I hope that this will develop into a profitable relationship for both of us.

❷   I thought it might be helpful to send you the enclosed information, which tells a little more about me and the works you will be displaying. Also, I am writing to summarize the arrangements we discussed informally. I trust you don't mind my putting this down in a letter and asking you to return a signed copy. Once I have received your signed copy, I will ship my works to your gallery. This bit of formality will help me feel that I have taken care of business matters and can concentrate on what I do best—my art!

❸   The ___ works of mine that you have chosen for your exhibition are tagged on the back so that you can easily identify them. They are as follows:

    1. Title, date, and dimensions: _____.
       We have agreed on a retail price of $_____ for this work.
    2. Title, date, and dimensions:_____.
       We have agreed on a retail price of $_____ for this work.
    3. Title, date, and dimensions:_____.
       We have agreed on a retail price of $_____ for this work.
    4. Title, date, and dimensions:_____.
       We have agreed on a retail price of $_____ for this work.
    5. Title, date, and dimensions:_____.
       We have agreed on a retail price of $_____ for this work.
    6. Title, date, and dimensions:_____.
       We have agreed on a retail price of $_____ for this work.

❹   We have also agreed that you will take a _(50)_ percent commission on the sale of each of these works, payable within _(30)_ days of the sale. Because you and I have not yet established a permanent business relationship, I must ask that you pay me a full _(50)_ percent of the selling price, even if you do not receive full payment from a client who takes possession of my work. I understand that it is your practice to offer a (10) percent discount to a limited number of preferred clients, and I accept that this practice may result in my receiving proportionally less for my works.

❺   For my inventory records, I would appreciate receiving the names and addresses of the persons or corporations that purchase my art, so that I might contact them in the future either to borrow the works back for an exhibition or to rephotograph them.

❻   In the event that works do not sell by the closing dates of the exhibition, _____, I would appreciate your sending them back to me in the crates in which they were delivered. The expense of shipping and insuring the works that are returned to me will be paid by
_____(DEALER'S NAME)_____. The expense of _____(FRAMING)_____ will be covered by
_____(YOUR NAME)_____.

     I certainly hope the collectors who visit your gallery respond favorably to my art and that you will be interested in exhibiting my work again in the future. I would appreciate your keeping me in mind when you are organizing future theme shows or considering new choices for the gallery's regular roster of artists.

     Assuming you are in agreement with what I have described in this letter, I would appreciate your signing the enclosed copy and returning it to me in the self-addressed envelope. If there are any points that need further discussion or clarification, please give me a call or drop me a note.

     Again, I am glad to have my art displayed in your gallery as part of a terrific exhibition. Thank you for your interest in my work.

Sincerely yours,

ACKNOWLEDGED:

_____
SIGNATURE   DATE
_____
TITLE

YOUR NAME
YOUR ADDRESS
CITY, STATE, ZIP
PHONE AND/OR FAX

Sending Prints or Reproductions to Galleries

WHEN TO USE THIS LETTER

If, like many artists, you find yourself in the business of selling limited-edition prints or reproductions, you can wind up servicing dozens of galleries around the country, some of which you may never visit. The problem in managing this kind of business is that, with so little personal contact and such limited numbers of retail sales per gallery, both you and the dealer can easily neglect one another. It is important, therefore, to have accurate records of your activities with the gallery and a firm understanding of who does what when. The purpose of this letter is to establish that kind of understanding.

If possible, it would be better to *sell* the dealer the reproductions, rather than to offer them on consignment, for it can become quite difficult and costly to recover work or to collect on an unpaid bill. This is particularly the case when the amount is not large and the dealer lives a good distance away. Even if you feel obliged to take that risk when you are beginning or expanding your business activities, try to get to the point where galleries have to buy work outright.

In selling limited-editions, keep in mind that many states (New York, California, and Illinois among them) require the artist, publisher, and/or dealer to provide detailed information about the number of prints or reproductions published, including any publisher's proofs and artist's proofs.

IMPORTANT POINTS TO CONSIDER

Paragraph ❸

Make sure you identify in every way possible the work you are releasing to the dealer. Enter titles, dates, dimensions, edition numbers, and any other markings that would help to certify what you have delivered, should a problem ever arise.

If you send some works framed and others unframed, if some items are reproductions and others are original works, or if some prints are new issues while others are from sold-out editions, you may wish to spell out these different features in the space provided.

If you anticipate a greater degree of complexity with respect to these matters, you may want to modify this letter and deal with the costs of packing, insuring, and shipping in a separate paragraph.

Paragraph ❹

This sample shows some standard terms filled in, but if the dealers wish to show only a few relatively inexpensive prints or reproductions, you may be able to convince them to buy the pieces outright rather than take them on consignment. You may also want to establish a minimum amount of work that they must handle in order to justify the time and effort you will expend in servicing their gallery. That is, you could establish a policy that a gallery must buy a certain number, or up to a certain dollar volume, in order to represent you. Of course, these options would entail your modifying this paragraph.

Paragraph ❺

It will become very easy for you and the dealer to neglect one another, so you should establish a relatively short time frame during which this agreement will be in effect. Six months usually suffices to determine whether the dealer will be able to sell your work, unless he or she is in a resort community and has not yet offered your work during the resort's peak season.

Paragraph ❻

This refers to any biographical or professional material you will be sending to help support the sale of your artwork. The intention here is to be as helpful as possible, but you are also establishing the value of the literature, videotapes, or other material you are making available to the dealer.

Date

Dealer's Name
Gallery Name
Street Address
City, State, Zip

Dear _____ :

Thank you for the interest you expressed recently regarding limited editions of my work. I would very much like to sell these through your gallery, and I hope that this will be the start of a profitable relationship between us.

I am writing to review some of the topics we discussed, just to be sure that I clearly understand how we will be working together. If my recollection is in any way inaccurate, please let me know immediately. If, on the other hand, you agree with the points covered in this letter, I would appreciate your signing the enclosed copy and returning it to me for my records.

❸ You have asked me to send you _____ copies each of _____ limited-edition works. Specifically, you are interested in the works listed here:

Title_____ (____ × _____ ", retail price $_____)
Other features: _____
Title_____ (____ × _____ ", retail price $_____)
Other features: _____
Title_____ (____ × _____ ", retail price $_____)
Other features: _____
Title_____ (____ × _____ ", retail price $_____)
Other features: _____
Title_____ (____ × _____ ", retail price $_____)
Other features: _____
Title_____ (____ × _____ ", retail price $_____)
Other features: _____

I will be glad to cover the cost of packing, insuring, and shipping these works to your gallery.

❹ We have agreed that you will take a (50) percent commission on the sale of these prints/reproductions, with the balance due me within (30) days of any sale. The retail prices may not be discounted, and I will expect to receive my (50) percent of the purchase price within (30) days after a client takes possession of a work, even if the client has not paid in full.

❺ In the event that one or more of these works does not sell within (6) months of your receipt of the work, I will expect you either to return the unsold items or to purchase them from me at (50) percent of the retail price.

❻ Please review the biographical materials that I have included, which I hope will be helpful to you. I do ask that you return the _____ to me in good condition.

Again, I'm very pleased to have these limited editions of my work made available through your gallery. I hope they sell quickly and that you and I can discuss making more of my work available to your clients. Please let me know if you have any questions or concerns.

Sincerely yours,

YOUR NAME
YOUR ADDRESS
CITY, STATE, ZIP
PHONE AND/OR FAX

ACKNOWLEDGED:

_____
SIGNATURE   DATE

_____
TITLE

Agreeing to Exhibit in a Business Establishment: Banks, Restaurants, Office Lobbies, etc.

WHEN TO USE THIS LETTER

William M. Harnett (1848-92), whose *trompe l'oeil* paintings were exhibited in 1992 at New York's Metropolitan Museum of Art, made his name by exhibiting his pictures in department stores, factories, restaurants, and industrial fairs. He built a career without having to gain the support of gallery owners or museum curators.

Today, it is common for artists to take advantage of semi-public spaces that are adequate for small exhibitions. The locations may not be as prestigious or professional-looking, but they are probably visited by more people than a commercial gallery. Because the normal business of a restaurant, bank, or office lobby has nothing to do with the exhibition and sale of artwork, an artist has to assume that artwork will receive only a minimum of care and attention while on display in these locations. Therefore, some basic agreement needs to be made with the person who either owns or manages the space.

Before accepting an invitation to exhibit in this kind of semi-public space, consider whether the galleries that represent you would object to the idea, either because they think it demeans your work or because they believe they would lose sales.

IMPORTANT POINTS TO CONSIDER

Paragraph ②

The critical issue in this paragraph is to establish who is actually authorized and/or willing to sign a letter of agreement. It may take several letters to reach an owner, building manager, or bank vice president willing to put his or her signature on the letter.

Paragraph ③

It is best to establish a time frame for your exhibit, even if the manager of the space doesn't give you the specific dates. You don't want your work to become a permanent part of the decor. Any sales or commission opportunities are most likely to come in the first month or two of the exhibit. After that point, people begin to assume that the art belongs there.

Paragraph ④

Providing a sign and brochures or other information, along with price lists, will explain the presence of your artwork and encourage people to buy it. Also, you will relieve employees of the business from having to answer queries on your behalf. Just make sure the manager approves of your plans.

Provide as much information as possible to potential customers. Some businesses—particularly those that are nonprofit—may not want the exhibition of your work to be obviously commercial, so in those situations, you may need to forgo the sign, the brochures, and so on and strike a few words from the letter. It still might be possible to leave a guest book out so that you can contact the people who sign in when they visit.

Even if it seems clear to everyone that the establishment will not be taking a commission on sales, the terms of that agreement need to be stated in this paragraph.

Paragraph ⑤

While it is unlikely that the host business will insure your artwork, make sure to ask and then alter the first sentence of this paragraph accordingly.

You may, for some reason, need access to your pictures during the run of the exhibition, and this paragraph establishes that need. Also, you may plan an opening reception or private tours for family and collectors, or you may need to substitute works as some of them are sold; this allows for the owner or manager to know that in advance.

Date

Name of the Owner or Manager
Name of the Establishment
Street Address
City, State, Zip

Dear _____:

I am delighted to have the opportunity to exhibit my artwork in your space and, again, I thank you for making this display possible. You are performing a great service to me and, I hope, to the people of the community who see my works as a result.

❷ I want to confirm the dates and arrangements we discussed so that I am clear about both my obligations and the services being provided by you. If any of the points I cover in this letter are not completely accurate, or if you would prefer that someone else associated with the space review this agreement, I would appreciate your letting me know right away. Otherwise, I would ask that you please sign the enclosed copy of this letter and return it to me for my records.

❸ You have kindly made available the dates of _____ through _____, 19____, for the exhibition of my artwork. The exact number and placement of works will be determined when I deliver and install them on _____.

❹ Knowing that the employees working near the exhibition will be busy with their responsibilities, I will provide signs and information for customers and will handle inquiries and sales by myself. The information will include some biographical facts, my address and phone number, and the titles, dates, dimensions, and prices of the artwork. It's my understanding that you are not expecting any payment for the use of the space or a commission on any sales that take place as a result of the exhibition.

❺ I understand that you will / will not insure my artworks while on display. I would appreciate every effort being made to protect them from damage or theft. For my own insurance purposes, I may want to photograph the works while they are on display in your space. I will notify you of other access that I may need, to show or sell my work.

 I will also make arrangements to remove the artworks after the last day of the exhibition, and I will take away any signs and remaining copies of the information I provided.

 Again, thank you for giving me this opportunity to exhibit my artwork.

Sincerely yours,

YOUR NAME
YOUR ADDRESS
CITY, STATE, ZIP
PHONE AND/OR FAX

ACKNOWLEDGED:

_____
SIGNATURE   DATE

_____
TITLE

Confirming Gallery Representation Within a Limited Geographic Area

WHEN TO USE THIS LETTER

Fewer and fewer artists are relying on one dealer to sell their work. In the past, an artist would entrust his or her business affairs entirely to one gallery, often receiving a monthly advance against sales. Now it is more common to exhibit major oil paintings with one gallery in New York, and another in Chicago and Los Angeles, and at the same time to have works on paper (prints, watercolors, monotypes, etc.) available at galleries in St. Louis, Houston, San Francisco, Palm Beach, and Seattle.

This situation can lead to difficulties, and it is in the artist's interest to be clear and honest with any dealer interested in representing him or her. Furthermore, it is important to clarify the limit of the dealer's ability to represent the artist, for without such clarification the dealer might be able to claim a commission on sales of work to collectors living or working near the gallery, even though the dealer was not directly involved in the transaction. This letter will help in that effort.

As implied earlier, the problems that may arise between you and a dealer who shows *some* of your artwork could involve ethical as well as legal considerations. Make sure you are guided by what is fair, reasonable, and honest.

IMPORTANT POINTS TO CONSIDER

Paragraphs ❸ and ❹

These two paragraphs make clear that, while you are offering the dealer the opportunity to sell your artwork, you are not giving him or her an exclusive geographic sales territory. Paragraph 3 establishes *why* you do not want to grant exclusive rights; and Paragraph 4 explains that a dealer who represents you in another city may very well have clients near this new gallery. These two parts of the letter should help avoid potential conflicts.

The second sentence in Paragraph 4 should allay any concerns the dealer may have about your intentions to sell directly to his or her clients—that's a reasonable concern for a dealer to have when an artist asks for a nonexclusive agreement.

One art consultant strongly suggested that the last sentence of this paragraph be struck out. "Don't volunteer to send prospective buyers to the gallery until you see how the gallery works for you. An artist should be able to sell directly to clients with whom there already is an established relationship."

Paragraph ❺

In this paragraph, the point is to establish what the dealer has agreed to, what you are sending, and who will be responsible for making the artwork ready to display (including framing of pictures). If the dealer has offered to cover any or all of these expenses, by all means agree to it. In all likelihood, however, you will have to bear the burden of making your work available for sale at the gallery.

Paragraph ❻

Here is where you begin to face the most difficult part of the artist/dealer relationship: getting paid. Too often, dealers withhold money from artists after paintings have been sold. Sometimes their excuse is that they have received partial payment from the client and don't want to pay the artist until all the money has been received. Other times the dealer thinks it is his or her prerogative to pay all the gallery's monthly business expenses first and then divide the remainder (if there is any) among the artists whose work has sold.

Even if you and the gallery owner haven't actually discussed payment terms (like those suggested in this sample), this paragraph will show the recipient that there are reasonable expectations for you to have, even if he or she hadn't expected to pay in as timely and reasonable a fashion.

Paragraph ❼

It is reasonable to assume that if a dealer can sell your artwork, he or she will do so within twelve months. If that doesn't happen, you are better off taking your work back before it is lost or damaged. This paragraph will let the dealer know you want something to happen while your artwork is in his or her possession.

Date

Name of Gallery Director
Title
Name of Gallery
Street Address
City, State, Zip

Dear _____:

I am very pleased to have talked to you about showing my artwork in your gallery. I look forward to working with you and your staff and hope this will become a very profitable relationship for everyone.

Just so I am clear about the various matters we discussed, I will briefly review our discussion here. If my recollections are not completely accurate, I would appreciate your letting me know. Otherwise, please sign a copy of this letter and return it to me at your earliest convenience.

❸ As you know, I have enjoyed a supportive relationship with dealers in other parts of the country. I want to maintain those business associations while taking advantage of the opportunity you are offering. For that reason, I want to make it clear that the agreement between us is not exclusive and that I will be free to exhibit and sell my work through galleries in other cities.

❹ Art collectors do buy from dealers located in different cities, and galleries often sell to clients outside their geographic locations, but to the extent possible, I will not offer my artwork through other galleries or agents who actively sell artwork in your area on a regular basis. I will not sell directly to any individuals or corporations based in your city but will refer those prospective clients to you.

❺ We discussed your including several of my artworks in group shows and then, perhaps, presenting a solo exhibition of my work, and we decided _____ _____. I am happy with that arrangement and will send you the works we discussed. I will crate, ship, and insure them at __(MY)__ expense and will forward an inventory list of the titles, dates, dimensions, and retail prices for your records. If there is any problem with this shipment, I would appreciate your letting me know immediately.

❻ We have agreed that you will take a _(50)_ percent commission on the sale of any of my works, and that the balance will be due to me within _(30)_ days of the sale. While I recognize that you may wish to extend discounts and/or a schedule of payment terms to your clients, I do ask that you pay my _(50)_ percent of the retail price of any sold artwork within _(30)_ days of the date when a client takes possession of it.

❼ I think it would be best for us to establish a time frame for our business agreement. I suggest that we reevaluate our agreement after ____(ONE YEAR)____ to determine whether it has been mutually beneficial and is worth continuing. Unless you have objections, I will assume that our agreement will be in effect for ____(ONE YEAR)____ from the date of this letter.

Sincerely yours,

ACKNOWLEDGED:

_____   _____
SIGNATURE   DATE

_____
TITLE

YOUR NAME
YOUR ADDRESS
CITY, STATE, ZIP
PHONE AND/OR FAX

13

Committing to Exclusive Representation by a Gallery

WHEN TO USE THIS LETTER

Even though the art market has become quite diversified, gallery owners still want to be the exclusive agents for their most successful artists. They feel that if they are going to promote an artist's name and professional standing, the gallery should participate in the rewards that accrue from that effort.

Both the gallery and the artist should understand just how far-reaching the word "exclusive" can be, and this letter is designed to identify a few of the rights and responsibilities attached to that word. In all likelihood, this letter will be revised several times before it is signed and countersigned. The point is to find some agreement on what each party is giving and taking from the relationship.

Make sure you review the matter of consignment laws (see the introductory section of the book) when preparing a letter like this one. You should understand that while state laws may protect your artwork from potential claims made by the gallery's creditors, these laws vary from state to state and are often difficult to enforce.

One major difficulty with an exclusive arrangement is that, more than any other type of agreement, it ties the artist to the dealer without a way to alter the situation during the fixed term. This could have a substantial impact on the income of the artist, since there is no assurance that the relationship will lead to sales or that the work will be effectively promoted.

One way to deal with this problem is to provide for a minimum amount to be paid to the artist during a given period. If that amount is not paid, the relationship, by its own terms, dissolves. This can be effected in a number of ways. One way is to provide that the gallery will pay an amount each month to the artist as an advance against sales. The second way is to provide that if, after a certain period of time, the artist has not received an account from the gallery of sales totaling a specified dollar amount (at the minimum), the agreement terminates. In that case, it is probably a good idea to provide that the artist *may* terminate the relationship with 30 days' notice.

IMPORTANT POINTS TO CONSIDER

Paragraph ❷

The key points in the first sentence are that the gallery and the artist must both agree on the pricing of artwork, and that the gallery is entitled to a commission on the sale of all the artist's work during the period of this agreement.

It is important to establish that the dealer is not entitled to a commission when you give artwork to a family member, merchant, or charitable organization—which artists do all the time. This would include works that you have used in barter for goods and services, even though you are receiving something of monetary value for them.

Another important point to consider is whether you are appointing your gallery as your *exclusive agent only*, or as your agent with *exclusive power to sell*. If the former, you would have the legal right to sell works yourself and not be legally obligated to pay a commission to the agent; if the latter, you would not be legally permitted to make a sale without paying the gallery the agreed-upon commission. You should emend the second sentence accordingly.

Paragraph ❸

If you have a fairly steady flow of monthly payments from the gallery, you may want to strike out the sentence about partial payments and ask only for timely payments once clients of the gallery have paid in full. That will simplify the paperwork for both you and the dealer.

Paragraph ❹

This one paragraph covers several of the most difficult issues in the relationship between an artist and a dealer: discounting, sales by a third party, and the identity of collectors. Most galleries routinely discount prices but don't want to publicize that fact. They often work with other gallery owners to sell work, but don't like splitting the commission. And some dealers withhold the identity of their clients out of fear that the artist or another gallery will start selling artwork to them.

Before you send this letter, learn the dealer's views on these issues. You may need to reword this paragraph, which takes a fairly standard approach. You may have to drop those prerogatives that he or she adamantly opposes. On the other hand, you may be persuasive enough to win the dealer's acceptance of the terms you prefer.

Paragraph ❺

There are two questions you may want to resolve in your discussions with the dealer before sending the letter: Do you, or does the dealer, pay for the framing of pictures; and who covers the expense of shipping work to the gallery? There is space in this paragraph to fill in concerning agreements of this kind. Considering that either the framing or the shipping could be quite substantial expenses (with frames easily totaling thousands of dollars), you may want to suggest sharing the expense. If you don't pay for the framing, you may want the dealer to deduct that cost from the retail price before taking his or her commission. Otherwise, the dealer will be earning a commission on the sale of your frame.

You should also determine what the dealer will do in announcing and opening exhibitions; you may choose to share the cost of a color reproduction on the announcement, of a catalog for the show, or of a dinner for selected clients after the opening.

Paragraph ❻

Here again you will need to have a conversation about how often the dealer normally exhibits an artist's work. Most galleries present solo shows every two to three years, depending on how prolific the artist is.

Paragraph ❼

If your relationship with the gallery runs smoothly—sales are steady and you get reports on a regular basis—then this part of the agreement will become unnecessary. On the other hand, it will become important to you if the gallery doesn't live up to its agreement, for it will help you apply a measurable standard to the gallery's performance.

Date

Name of Gallery Owner
Name of Gallery
Street Address
City, State, Zip

Dear _____:

I have given a good deal of thought to the matters we recently discussed, and I am writing to review the main points of our discussion in this letter. Before I do that, however, I must say again that I am very pleased I am to be offered exclusive representation by your gallery. It is an opportunity that will be, I hope, profitable for both of us for years to come. The arrangement does call for each of us to make commitments to the other, and I want to clarify those as we establish a formal agreement.

❷ The retail price of my artwork will be established by mutual consent, and the gallery will receive a _____ percent commission on the sale of any and all artwork that I have created or will create for as long as our agreement is in effect. This will include sales by you only/sales by me, and sales to my existing clients, as well as those who purchase my work through your gallery. We have agreed that you will not be due a commission on any artwork that I give free of charge to family members, charitable organizations, or public institutions, even if these are subsequently sold by the recipient. Furthermore, you will not have any claim on works created during the period our agreement is in effect that are not sold during that same period.

❸ We have agreed that I will receive _____ percent of the retail price for any of my artwork sold while our agreement is in effect, payable within (30) days of your receiving all or part of the total retail price. In the event that a client makes partial payment, you will send me _____ percent of the monies received within (30) days until such time as the full amount is paid.

❹ Knowing that it is customary for you to offer a (10) percent discount to preferred customers, I agree that in those situations I will be paid my standard _____ percent on the discounted retail price. Any further discounts will be absorbed by your gallery. If the artwork is sold through another gallery or agent, you will split the dealer's commission, and I will receive _____ percent of the retail selling price. No matter how my artwork is sold, I will receive the names and addresses of the individuals, corporations, or institutions purchasing that work.

❺ It will be my responsibility to create the artwork, deliver it to the gallery, and pay all the expenses related to those activities. Additionally, I agree to do the following:_____
_____.
The gallery will be responsible for presenting, insuring, and promoting the sale of that artwork and handling the related business matters. The gallery will pay the expenses associated with those activities, including the cost of advertising the exhibitions, mailing exhibition announcements, and providing refreshments at openings. Additionally, the gallery agrees to do the following: _____
_____.

❻ Like any other artist, I am eager for my artwork to be seen by as many people as possible, and I want to be sure that I have opportunities to present a solo exhibition at least once every ____ year(s) and to participate in group exhibitions at least once every _____. I will expect the gallery to exhibit my artwork with that kind of frequency and make it available for viewing by prospective clients at all times.

❼ I suggest that we consider our agreement in effect for a period of _____ and that we review the progress of our relationship every _____. I will assume that is agreeable to you unless you suggest another time frame.

I believe that covers the most important points relating to our proposed business relationship. If I have forgotten anything, or if I have not outlined the agreement as you believe it should exist, I would appreciate your letting me know as soon as possible. If, on the other hand, you are in agreement with me on these matters, please sign the enclosed copy and return it to me at your earliest convenience.

Sincerely yours,

ACKNOWLEDGED:

_____   Your Name
NAME   DATE   Your Address
_____   City, State, Zip
TITLE   Phone and/or Fax

15

Granting Permission to Reproduce Your Artwork in a Magazine, Book, or Calendar

HOW TO USE THIS LETTER

This and the next two letters will help you control one of your most valuable assets, the copyright to the images you create. Copyright can be a very complicated subject, and there are lengthy books that define what a copyright is, who owns it, and how it becomes transferred. For the purpose of this letter, we assume that you created the picture and therefore own the copyright to the image.

The most likely request you will receive is from the publisher of a magazine, book, or calendar who wants to use your picture free of charge. Assuming that the promotional value is sufficient to grant this request, you will want to send a letter with your transparencies establishing several important concerns.

If you are asked to send original artwork so that the publisher can photograph it or generate color separations directly from it, then in the second paragraph of this letter you need to make the publisher responsible for any loss or damage to the artwork. The last two sentences in the third paragraph should also reflect that you are sending original artwork.

IMPORTANT POINTS TO CONSIDER

Paragraph ❷

The first two sentences describe the material you are sending. You should insert the number of photographs, and you might also attach a caption sheet, so that you establish the number of transparencies that are to be returned to you.

It is unlikely the publisher will ask you to suggest corrections on the color proofs, but you should extend the offer.

Paragraph ❸

This is the most important paragraph and the real reason for sending a letter. Even though the copyright laws now presume that the artist maintains his or her rights—even after the artwork has been sold or published in some other form—the safest thing to do is serve notice that you own those rights.

It is a good idea to let the publisher know your photographs are valuable and that you want them back, and then to follow up with a request for their return after the magazine, book, or calendar has been published.

Paragraph ❹

Most publishers will gladly send you two free copies of the publication in which your artwork appears, so don't hesitate to ask for them. If you think you might have use for additional copies, find out if you can buy them at a discounted price.

Date

Name of Editor, Publisher, or Art Director
Title
Name of Publishing Company
Street Address
City, State, Zip

Dear _____;

This letter is a follow-up to the conversation we recently had regarding your interest in publishing my artwork in your forthcoming _____.
I am delighted to have my work become a part of this publication, and I thank you for the request.

❷   I am enclosing _____ accurate photographs of the works you expressed interest in, each marked as to the title, date, dimensions, ownership, and gallery credit. These are professionally made photographs with color bars included next to the art, and they should allow you to get an accurate reproduction. If you have any questions about that accuracy, I would be happy to look over color proofs of the separations and indicate any color corrections that might improve the presentation.

❸   I have two important requests to make. The first is that you publish a caption with any reproduction of my artwork indicating that I own the copyright to the images. If you put the words "Copyright © 19___ by _____(YOUR NAME)_____
_____" as close to the reproduction as possible, that will be fine. My second request is that you return the photographs to me as soon as you have finished using them. They are quite valuable, as you know, and I need to have them returned.

❹   I would very much like to have copies of your publication to share with friends and collectors, and I would appreciate your sending me __(2)__ copies free of charge. I would also like to know how I might purchase additional discounted copies if I should need them in the future.

    If there is anything else you need for this project that I can help you with, please don't hesitate to get in touch with me. Again, many thanks for your interest in my work.

Sincerely yours,

YOUR NAME
YOUR ADDRESS
CITY, STATE, ZIP
PHONE AND/OR FAX

ACKNOWLEDGED:

_____
NAME   DATE
_____
TITLE

Allowing Publication of Reproductions Solely for Promotional Value

WHEN TO USE THIS LETTER

Artists are continually asked to lend, donate, or give their artwork to support a charitable organization, thereby gaining "valuable exposure." There are even some large commercial publishing companies that ask to publish posters or limited-edition reproductions of artists' work without paying for it, because of the "promotional value" to the artist. Most of these kinds of offers are not worthwhile opportunities, yet occasionally they prove valuable if the publicity generated is substantial and/or well targeted, or if the artist can use the reproductions for self-promotion. For example, one artist created a poster image for the New Orleans Symphony Orchestra and then mailed copies to her clients with an invitation to a gallery showing. The poster created a real interest in the artist's work and served as an endorsement of her talent.

This letter will be useful when someone from a publishing company, charitable institution, or social organization will be responsible for reproductions of your artwork. It tells them what you expect to have happen and how you want to participate in the quality-control process.

IMPORTANT POINTS TO CONSIDER

Paragraph ❷

A reproduction of a work of art will sometimes look like an entirely different image if the color separations and printing aren't done well. Colors and values can become totally distorted, and subtleties can become completely lost. The best way to ensure that reproductions of your work will be as accurate as possible is to evaluate both the proofs of the color separations and the choice of printing paper. While some technical knowledge would help in making judgments about these, you mainly need to be able to examine how the proof looks in comparison to your original work of art.

Paragraph ❸

While it is not absolutely necessary that your copyright notice appear on all copies of the reproduction, it is wise to include it as a warning to those who might infringe upon your rights.

Paragraph ❹

You should receive a quantity of free copies for your own use, whether you are paid for the project or not. The quantity will depend on the number of copies printed, but will usually fall between 20 and 200 copies. In your discussion with the publisher, make sure it is understood that you are free to give away or sell your copies as you see fit.

Date

Name of Publisher
Title
Name of Publishing Company
Street Address
City, State, Zip

Dear _____:

This letter is a follow-up to our recent conversation regarding your interest in publishing a reproduction of my artwork entitled _____ _____. I am very pleased that you want to reproduce my work in this manner, and I only want to clarify a few points regarding this.

❷   As I explained, my principal concern is the quality of the reproduction. For that reason, I will only grant permission to use my artwork so long as I have the right to approve the selection of printing paper and the proofs of the color separations. Furthermore, while I don't wish to make things difficult for you, I would like to be able to approve the printer's color proofs.

❸   Under those conditions, I hereby agree to give your company, _____ _____, the right to print _____ copies of my artwork on _____" × _____" sheets. Each of these prints will include my name, the title of the artwork, and the words "Copyright © 19___ by _____." No other use may be made
                                              (YOUR NAME)
of this or any other of my copyrighted artwork without my written permission.

❹   In exchange for my granting you this permission, you have agreed to give me _____ free copies of the reproduction, which I may sell or give away as I choose. Those copies will be shipped to my home address by the most efficient carrier.

        Thanks again for your interest. I look forward to working with you on this publication of my work.

                                        Sincerely yours,

                                        YOUR NAME
                                        YOUR ADDRESS
                                        CITY, STATE, ZIP
                                        PHONE AND/OR FAX

ACKNOWLEDGED:

_____   _____
SIGNATURE   DATE
_____
TITLE

Establishing a Royalty Arrangement with a Publisher

WHEN TO USE THIS LETTER

The poster and limited-edition reproduction markets are much larger than most artists imagine when they first become involved in them. Some artists whose names and images are well known will earn over a million dollars in royalties from the sale of their most popular published artwork. Given that potential, it is especially important for artists to have legally binding agreements with publishers before allowing reproductions to be made of their artwork.

Many publishers will have a standard boilerplate contract to offer an artist with whom they want to do business. But in the absence of such a contract, this letter will offer basic protection and define certain privileges an artist will want.

IMPORTANT POINTS TO CONSIDER

Paragraph ❷

It is important to know how many copies of the reproduction will be printed. Moreover, you may wish to set a limit on that number and to be able to renegotiate any aspect of this agreement once the market for your work has been tested. That is, if you sell 5,000 copies of a poster rather quickly and the publisher wants to reprint it, you may want to ask for a higher royalty percentage or have prints made from other works before you extend the original agreement.

Paragraph ❸

As discussed with Letter 7, the most important aspect of a publishing venture is the reproduction quality. The three factors which most affect quality are the color separations, the paper stock, and the printing itself. As an artist, you want to be involved in the quality control, and this paragraph makes that clear.

Paragraph ❹

The first sentence establishes the royalty percentage you will earn on the first prints or reproductions published. You may be able to increase that percentage if subsequent editions are published. The standard royalty earned on posters and limited-edition reproductions is 15 percent of the wholesale price, paid quarterly or semi-annually. The percentage will be higher on prints that you either hand-color or print yourself, and you may earn a higher percentage after a certain number of copies have been sold. A publisher will normally issue a check for those earnings, along with a computer-generated statement listing total sales (by source) for each item on which you earn royalties.

Paragraph ❺

With limited-edition reproductions or original prints, the artist receives a certain number of artist's proofs and is free to sell these, usually at a price slightly higher than that of the regular edition. Furthermore, the artist can either buy additional copies at less than the wholesale price or can negotiate to receive additional copies from the regular edition.

When the artist shares part of the production cost and is, effectively, a co-publisher, he or she may receive a percentage of the total commensurate with the percentage of the expenses he or she has paid.

Paragraph ❻

This paragraph lets the publisher know what you want to happen if the reproductions either sell out quickly or don't sell well. In the first situation, you will want the publisher to request permission to produce more and, perhaps, pay you a better royalty (since the production and sales costs will be lower and the sales are more certain). If the reproductions sell poorly or if the publisher goes out of business, you will want to make sure your images are not just dumped onto the market. In such an instance, this paragraph allows you to buy the unsold product for the amount of money the publisher invested in it.

Date

Name of Publisher
Title
Name of Publishing Company
Street Address
City, State, Zip

Dear _____:

Thank you for taking the time to discuss the details of our proposed publishing arrangement. It was helpful to review the various aspects of this business proposition, and I believe I have a clear understanding of how we will proceed. I am writing to summarize our agreement, and I would appreciate it if you would sign the enclosed copy of this letter if you agree with all the points covered. If there are any items that need further discussion or revision, please let me know.

❷ First, your company plans to publish reproductions of my artwork, entitled _____, as _____" × _____" prints. There will be an initial printing of _____ copies, with subsequent printings of copies to be discussed, depending on sales. These prints will be distributed through various channels of distribution.

❸ You have agreed that I will have the right to approve the selection of the paper on which the reproductions will be printed, the proofs of the color separations, and proofs from the printer each time that copies are printed. Furthermore, each copy will be printed with my name and a notice of my ownership of the copyright to the image. The notice will read: "Copyright © 19____ by _____(YOUR NAME)_____."

❹ I have agreed to accept a _(15)_ percent royalty payment for the sale of each print from the first printing (number). You have indicated this is the standard percentage earned by artists whose works you are currently publishing. I understand that I will receive a _____(QUARTERLY)_____ statement of sales activity and a check for the amount earned during that period.

❺ In addition, I will receive _____ copies free of charge and will have the option to buy additional copies at _____ for as long as they are in inventory. I may give these away, donate them to nonprofit organizations, or sell them for an amount of money not less than the current wholesale price.

❻ If, at any point, you should want to publish additional copies of this image, I will be happy to discuss that possibility with you and also reevaluate the royalty arrangement. If, on the other hand, you discontinue selling this print, I will have the opportunity to purchase any remaining copies at the manufacturing cost (the price paid for paper, color separations, and printing). These will be mine to use as I please.

I believe that covers all the points we discussed about this publishing project. If you feel we need to have further discussions regarding these or any other matters, please don't hesitate to call or drop me a line. Otherwise, I would appreciate your signing the enclosed copy of this letter and returning it to me at your earliest convenience.

I am eager to see my artwork reproduced as we've discussed and I thank you again for this exciting opportunity.

Sincerely yours,

YOUR NAME
YOUR ADDRESS
CITY, STATE, ZIP
PHONE AND/OR FAX

ACKNOWLEDGED:

_____
SIGNATURE   DATE
_____
TITLE

Hiring a Printer or Foundry to Reproduce Your Artwork

WHEN TO USE THIS LETTER

Most artists are not aware that, if someone makes casts of your sculpture, prints from your painting, etchings from your drawings, or textile prints based on your designs, that person is probably acquiring the copyright to the items that are based on your original work. The copyright laws have been interpreted to mean that if the people or company producing these prints, casts, or reproductions make a creative contribution to the process, then they own the copyright to what is termed the *derivative* work. That "creative contribution" may be as simple as adjusting the colors on the printing press, etching the metal plate, or applying the patina to the bronze cast.

This is little known because the companies that sell their printing and fabricating services to artists seldom exercise the rights and privileges that derive from this copyright ownership. It is possible, however, for a company to go into competition with their customers by selling the artist's prints or sculptures. And artists will find it difficult to initiate a lawsuit against someone who makes unauthorized use of their prints, casts, or reproductions unless they have the cooperation of the company which "created"— and therefore owns the rights to—the derivative works.

The best way to avoid potential problems is to have the printing company or foundry sign a letter of agreement establishing the exact services to be provided, the limits on their ability to use your artwork, and the transfer to you of the copyright. Many companies now have standard forms that can be used to transfer the copyright to the artist. If you get price quotations from several companies, ask if they have such a form. If they don't, or if the form they use seems inadequate, then use this letter.

IMPORTANT POINTS TO CONSIDER

Paragraph ❷

The intention here is to establish the basic details of the business arrangement. The paragraph should state what kinds of reproductions are being made (sculptures, posters, note cards, calendars, etc.), how many copies will be made, and the total cost for this work. The supplier may ask for a deposit or for the total amount with the order; you should state how much money you are sending with the letter and strike out the wording that does not apply.

Paragraph ❸

This paragraph makes it clear that the company does not have permission to reproduce your artwork in any other way or to sell reproductions to any other customers.

Paragraph ❹

Most businesses providing services to artists have a standard policy for dealing with the proofs or extra copies that are made in the process of creating the reproductions. Nevertheless, it is worth mentioning in this paragraph that you want the supplier either to destroy or send to you all proofs, and you want him or her to send you any extra copies that are made. The paragraph also allows the supplier to show examples of your job to another customer (or prospective customer).

Paragraph ❺

This may be the most important part of the letter; it asserts that the printer or foundry must transfer all rights in these reproductions—including that of copyright—directly to you. This one statement will clarify any potential confusion about the copyright to derivative material.

Date

Principal's Name
Name of Company
Street Address
City, State, Zip

Dear _____:

This letter sets forth the details of the agreement we discussed during our recent conversation. I would appreciate your reviewing the letter and returning a copy to me with your signature, acknowledging your acceptance of the terms.

❷   Your company, _____, will produce _____ sculptures/prints/posters/note cards/announcements reproducing my artwork, entitled _____, for a total price of $_____. I enclose a check for $_____, covering the deposit needed/the total amount, with $_____ due upon delivery to me of the finished items in satisfactory condition.

❸   With this agreement, I grant _____ a limited, nonexclusive license to make reproductions of my artwork solely for sale to me. This license is limited to the specific items and quantities mentioned in this letter and does not extend to any further reproduction of these images.

❹   You further agree either to destroy or send me any and all proofs which may be made in the production of these items, and you will send me any extra copies that are made. I agree to allow _____ to use some of these items as samples for the promotion of new business.

❺   Also, _____ agrees to transfer to me all rights to these reproduced items, including the copyright to the images derived from my artwork. Any reproduction of these images in sales literature, company brochures, exhibition catalogs, or other publications must carry a notice stating that I own the copyright.

      I look forward to working with you on this project.

Sincerely yours,

YOUR NAME
YOUR ADDRESS
CITY, STATE, ZIP
PHONE AND/OR FAX

ACKNOWLEDGED:

_____
SIGNATURE   DATE
_____
TITLE

Confirming a Portrait Commission Directly with a Client

WHEN TO USE THIS LETTER

Of the total number of portraits that are painted in a year's time, the majority will be arranged directly between the artist and his or her client (either the person to be painted or a relative). The details of size, clothing, price, and delivery date are usually discussed and agreed upon without signing a formal contract. The artist generally assumes that it is better to keep everything friendly and informal, while the client is often a bit nervous about what is supposed to happen. A letter stating what has been discussed will often ease the client and reassure the artist that his or her efforts will be rewarded.

IMPORTANT POINTS TO CONSIDER

Paragraph ❸

It is a good idea to include with this letter an outline of how you normally go about painting a portrait. Indicate when you will take photographs or do color studies; how many sessions you normally need with a client; how long those sessions will be and when they will be held; and whether you need to take clothing, jewelry, or furnishings to your studio.

You should also state that you will own all the sketches, photographs, and color studies you produce in preparing to paint the portrait. Though you may decide to sell or give that material to the client, start out by establishing that you own it.

Paragraph ❹

Artists have different ways of handling deposits for their commissions. Some ask for money to be sent with the signed letter of agreement and consider it to be nonrefundable. Others ask for nothing up front and expect payment only after the client has accepted the portrait.

Paragraph ❺

Most of the portrait painters who reviewed drafts of this letter said they would always give their clients an opportunity to cancel the commission at any stage of the project. That policy is reassuring to the reticent client and will make it more likely that the client will recommend your services to friends and family—something very important to the success of this business.

Accordingly, this letter has been written to give the client every assurance that he or she must be pleased with the portrait before paying for it. That does invite the possibility that the client will ask for an unreasonable number of changes, so it is helpful to state on the accompanying schedule of sittings that corrections will be made when the portrait is delivered to the client's home—the implication being that there is only one opportunity to suggest changes in the picture.

Date

Client's Name
Street Address
City, State, Zip

Dear _____:

As a follow-up to our recent conversation regarding a portrait of _____
_____, I want briefly to describe some of the arrangements
we have discussed. These will, I hope, set your mind at ease about how I plan to
go about creating this portrait and will clarify the time and financial commitments
I will need from you in order to do the best job possible.

     I am quite pleased to have this opportunity. We are furthering a great artistic
tradition, that of creating a portrait through the collaboration of a patron and an
artist. I hope this will prove to be as enjoyable for you as I know it will be for me,
and that this portrait will become something that is treasured for generations.

❸   After years of experience, I have learned that I create my best work when I
follow a schedule of sittings as described on the enclosed sheet. You'll see that I
have outlined the number and duration of the sittings, as well as my need to have
access to articles of clothing, jewelry, etc. Please note that in the course of these
sittings I will produce sketches, studies, and photographs and that I will retain
ownership of these. This schedule is, of course, a general outline, and I will work
out a specific plan that meets both our schedules.

❹   My fee for the portrait, at the size we have discussed, is $_____.
In keeping with standard professional practices, I ask that you give me a deposit of
_____ percent of that amount when we meet for the first sitting. The balance
of the money would be payable when you accept the completed portrait.

❺   People sometimes feel concerned about whether they will be pleased with
the portrait they have commissioned, and I want to assure you that I will make
every reasonable effort to create a work that satisfies you completely. If, in the
end, you are not completely satisfied with the portrait, you will be under no
obligation to accept it or pay the balance of the money. However, the deposit and
the artwork will be mine to keep if you choose not to accept the portrait.

     I will give you a call in a few days to answer any questions you may have
about this commission. Once you are comfortable with the arrangements we have
discussed, I would appreciate your sending me the enclosed copy of this letter
with your signature.

     I look forward to working with you.

Sincerely yours,

YOUR NAME
YOUR ADDRESS
CITY, STATE, ZIP
PHONE AND/OR FAX

ACKNOWLEDGED:

_____   _____
SIGNATURE   DATE
_____
TITLE

Establishing a Business Relationship with a Portrait Agent

HOW TO USE THIS LETTER

This letter establishes the basic relationship between an artist and the person or corporation that will earn a percentage of any portrait commission it negotiates. Some larger portrait brokerages draw up a separate letter of agreement for each commission they negotiate. The specifics of that particular portrait are written into the letter, and both client and artist are asked to sign it. Included in that agreement is the requirement that the client leave a deposit, which is held by the agent until the project is completed. In most cases, the deposit is refundable.

These project-by-project agreements do not define the ongoing relationship between the artist and the agent. Therefore a separate letter between these two defines their responsibilities and privileges.

Portrait agents generally represent a dozen or more artists whose portraits vary in style and price range. Invariably, three or four of those artists will get the most commissions negotiated by the agent, because the agent either finds their work best suited to a particular market or is more enthusiastic about their work. This letter shows that you are entering into this relationship because you want the agent to be active in promoting commissions for you, with the result that, eventually, you become one of his or her most successful artists.

IMPORTANT POINTS TO CONSIDER

Paragraph ❸

The agent will need to let prospective clients know how you go about creating a portrait, and the form described in this paragraph will accomplish that.

Paragraph ❹

The most common source of disagreement between artists and their agents is over the question of who actually secured a particular portrait commission. When more than one agent presents an artist's work, when a client waits years before deciding to commission a painting, or when a client who was once contacted by an agent later goes directly to the artist, it is sometimes difficult to decide who (if anyone) is entitled to the agent's commission.

Addressing the potential for conflicts, this paragraph states that the artist will strive to acknowledge the promotion done on his or her behalf. Most portrait artists feel it is important to decide in favor of the agent whenever there is a question of this sort.

Paragraph ❺

Several of the best-known portrait painters have been represented by the same agents for decades, but most other artists find they need periodically to review their relationships with agents. This paragraph establishes a specific time frame in which your portfolio is to be presented and commissions secured. This sample suggests a standard two-year agreement.

Date

Name of Agent
Name of Agent's Company
Street Address
City, State, Zip

Dear _____:

I valued our recent conversation about the possibility of having your company represent me as one of its portrait artists. It seems clear that this will work out to be a pleasant and profitable relationship between us. I sincerely appreciate your interest in my work and hope that we'll do a lot of business in the future.

I have been considering the best way for us to work together, while still allowing me to maintain the portrait business I have developed over the years on my own and with other representatives; it made sense to me to write down some of my concerns and needs. If you are in agreement that the points below could be the basis of our working relationship, then I would appreciate your signing a copy of this letter and returning it to me at your earliest convenience. If, on the other hand, you would like to discuss some of these matters further, please let me know.

❸ I mentioned that I have a standard form that I give to clients, which outlines how I go about painting a portrait. I am enclosing a copy of that form so you can see what I need in terms of the number of sessions with the client, how I handle photography, what I expect in terms of travel and accommodations, and so on.

❹ I have always enjoyed working with representatives and have made sure they received their commissions for the work I did for their clients. At the same time, a good portion of the work I do comes to me as a result of my own promotional efforts, or from referrals made by previous clients. Therefore, it should be our understanding that you will receive a commission only on portraits I do (1) for clients you bring to me or (2) for clients obtained as a direct result of recommendations made by people whose commissions you arranged for me. You will not be entitled to a commission on portraits for clients obtained as a result of my own or other agents' promotional efforts.

❺ I think it would be useful to establish a time frame for this agreement and then review our business relationship towards the end of that time. I suggest that the time period be ___(TWO YEARS)___ from the date of this letter.

If this letter accurately represents your understanding of our business relationship, I would appreciate your acknowledging that by signing a copy of this letter and returning it to me at your earliest convenience. If, on the other hand, there are matters that need further clarification, please let me know.

I look forward to working with you and your staff and appreciate this opportunity to have my portraits presented to your clients.

Sincerely yours,

YOUR NAME
YOUR ADDRESS
CITY, STATE, ZIP
PHONE AND/OR FAX

ACKNOWLEDGED:

_____
SIGNATURE   DATE
_____
TITLE

Defining the Stages of a Mural Commission

HOW TO USE THIS LETTER

The stark, minimal spaces that were popular in homes and offices of the 1960s and 1970s are less fashionable, and the preference among architects and interior designers is for decorative fabrics, furniture, and wall coverings. There is now a thriving industry of artists who are paid handsomely for murals, faux finishes, and artworks created to complement the designs of both interior and exterior spaces.

Because this can be a rather complicated business, in which a gallery owner, interior designer, architect, contractor, carpenter, electrician, and home owner can all become involved in the creation of one mural, it is important for an artist to have an agreement which clearly states what is expected of all those involved. This letter can be used to establish that agreement, either with an interior designer or with the owner of the space where the mural will be displayed.

The artists who reviewed this sample letter said they would find it particularly useful if the commission was for a painting that would be difficult to sell to another client, or if the price of the painting was over $500. A verbal agreement would be adequate if the completed painting could easily be sold to another client.

IMPORTANT POINTS TO CONSIDER

Paragraph ❸

It is important to get as many facts and figures into the paragraph as will accurately define what you are expected to create, how you will do it, and by what date it is to be completed. If you can think of any other details, add them to the letter so that there won't be any confusion about your project.

Paragraph ❹

The artists who reviewed this letter emphasized that the color sketch is very important to the success of a mural project. It can be a rough colored-pencil sketch, a painting done over a photocopy of a drawing, or a small oil painting on canvas. It is the best way to resolve differences that might exist between the client and the artist. The point is to give the client a good indication of how the mural will ultimately look; the client may request specific changes or approve the design. Some artists ask that their clients initial the final sketch to certify their approval.

Paragraph ❺

Most architects and interior designers recognize the value of an artist's time and will understand that you want to be paid for having developed a color sketch if it proves to satisfy their expectations. On the other hand, a private individual may not have confidence in his or her ability to judge the appearance of the final mural on the basis of the sketch. In those situations, it may be necessary to strike out the last sentence in this paragraph.

Paragraph ❻

Again, the point is to let the client know as much as possible about your needs as an artist. If those needs present any problem, this is the time to resolve them, if feasible.

Paragraph ❼

Some artists exclude expenses related to delivering and installing a mural if they won't be handling those jobs themselves. If other individuals or companies need to be hired to transport and mount the work, the cost may be difficult to determine at the outset; for example, the mural can take longer than expected to complete. If the client initiates changes that expand the project, it could become more difficult and expensive to install. Thus, you may need to alter the wording shown here.

Paragraph ❽

Your preparatory material will travel between you and the client during the negotiations related to this project, and it is therefore important to remind the client that you consider these to be your valuable property. Otherwise, the client might assume that he or she is entitled to have all the material related to the project. Moreover, this asserts that the copyright belongs to you.

Date

Name
Street Address
City, State, Zip

Dear _____:

I found our recent discussion to be informative and helpful, and I appreciate having gotten more information about the mural you wish to have created for _____ _(THE OWNER OF THE SPACE)_ . I'm excited about this project and appreciate the opportunity to be part of it.

Just to be sure we both understand the terms and conditions under which I might be creating this mural, I thought it would be helpful to review the items we covered in our recent discussion. If it occurs to you that I have not covered all the important aspects of this project, or that my recollection of the conversation is not completely accurate, please let me know as soon as possible. If, on the other hand, you feel this letter is an accurate summary of our agreement, I would appreciate your signing a copy and returning it to me.

❸ You have established that you want a mural on the subject of _____ _____ to be executed in _____ , measuring _____ × _____. It will be attached to a wall in or at _____ _____. The mural must have the following features, details, or motifs: _____ _____ You would like to have the mural completed and installed by _____.

❹ I have agreed to do a color sketch of my idea(s) so that you have a clear notion of the artwork I propose to create. This sketch will be fairly rough, but will be made to the scale of the finished mural and will be accurate enough to give you a clear idea of the overall composition. I expect to be able to deliver the sketch by _____, at which time we can discuss any changes you think might improve the final artwork.

❺ It is in our best interest to resolve any potential problems at this stage, and I will be happy to make revisions in the color sketch or to create a new sketch, if that will help us reach agreement about the final appearance of the mural. Because of the time and creative energy involved in developing these sketches, I will consider your initial deposit to be nonrefundable after you approve the color sketch.

❻ After receiving your approval of the color sketch, I will need _____ months to complete the mural, and I anticipate that I would need _____ days to install the mural.

❼ The total cost of the mural will be $_____, with a ___ percent deposit of $_____ due with this agreement, and the balance due on completion of the project. This fee will/will not include the expenses for the artwork and for transportation to and installation at the site.

❽ Any and all drawings, sketches, color studies, or photographs that I use in creating this mural will be mine to keep, and I will retain the copyright to those preparatory works as well as the final image of the mural, unless we negotiate a separate agreement for the transfer of that copyright.

Again, my thanks to you for giving me the opportunity to work on this exciting project.

Sincerely yours,

YOUR NAME
YOUR ADDRESS
CITY, STATE, ZIP
PHONE AND/OR FAX

ACKNOWLEDGED:

_____
SIGNATURE   DATE
_____
TITLE

Establishing a Commission to Create Artwork

HOW TO USE THIS LETTER

There are times when collectors have very specific expectations, and the only way they get exactly what they want is to commission a work from an artist. Their requirements might involve the size of the work, the subject, or even the style of the work. The more specific those requirements are, the more important it becomes for the artist to receive some assurance that the collector will actually purchase the commissioned work. Without that assurance, the artist may waste his or her time creating something no one else will want.

Several of the artists who reviewed this letter indicated that they seldom accept commissions because they don't like painting on demand. But in cases where the commission is attractive, or pressure from the dealer or collector is hard to resist, an artist would use this letter to clarify the stages involved in defining and executing the commission.

IMPORTANT POINTS TO CONSIDER

Paragraph ❷
The intention of this paragraph is to define the commission as clearly as possible; there should be no confusion about size, subject matter, and the ultimate site for the work.

Paragraph ❸
Problems will occur if the client has one conception of the final work and the artist has another. It would be helpful to use an existing work as a model, and you should create a color sketch that roughly indicates the proportions and content of the finished work of art.

Paragraph ❹
The review process described in this paragraph should make it possible to resolve differences or to terminate the project before the artist does an extensive amount of work. It is important to understand what options the client will have, and what commitment will need to be made after this review.

Paragraph ❺
This paragraph gives the client specific information about pricing, schedule of payments, and timing for the project, again with the intention of clarifying expectations.

Date

Name
Street Address
City, State, Zip

Dear _____:

Concerning our recent conversation about the possibility of creating a work of art for you, I am certainly pleased by your interest in such a project. In order to go further with this idea, it would be helpful to me to state here what you have requested, the time frame for this commission, and the financial terms that we might agree to.

❷ You have indicated you would like to have a _____ work on the subject of _____ for display in or at your _____ _____. It will have the following specific features: _____ _____
The completed artwork would measure _____ × _____ and would be displayed by _____ , 19____.

❸ In a situation like this, it is common practice for an artist to prepare a color sketch of an idea for a commissioned work and then have the client either approve the sketch or suggest changes. I propose to make a rough color sketch of my design, in scale with the size of the final work. Though the sketch would not be as detailed or refined as the final artwork, it would be clear enough to indicate the overall composition.

❹ Because I want you to be satisfied with the artwork you commission, I will be happy to discuss changes in the color sketch and, if necessary, will create revised sketches. If, after reviewing these various sketches you are not completely satisfied, you can cancel the project without any obligation. On the other hand, if you approve a final color sketch and want me to proceed, then to begin working I will need a nonrefundable deposit of _____ percent of the total price of the work.

❺ The total price of the commission will be $_____. Assuming you do approve the color sketch and give me a deposit, then the balance would be due on delivery. I anticipate that it would take me approximately _____ weeks/months to complete the work after you approve the color sketch.

I look forward to this project, and I'm eager to begin work on the sketch. I do wish to make sure I have clearly stated your ideas on the commission and would like to get your response to this letter. If you have any further thoughts about the artwork, please let me know. If what I have described here seems accurate, and you are in agreement about the terms of the commission, then I would appreciate your signing the enclosed copy of the letter and returning it to me at your earliest convenience.

Sincerely yours,

Your Name
Your Address
City, State, Zip
Phone and/or Fax

ACKNOWLEDGED:

_____
SIGNATURE   DATE
_____
TITLE

31

Model Release

HOW TO USE THIS LETTER

Unlike the other letters in this book, this one has a rather formal structure and uses standard legal terminology. There is no effort being made to sound friendly or casual. The reason is that you must convey to the person who will be modeling for you the clear sense that he or she is transferring certain rights in a legally binding agreement. There should be no confusion about this, and the language of the agreement emphasizes that point.

IMPORTANT POINTS TO CONSIDER

Paragraph ❶

The issue of photography may need further clarification if the model is concerned that photographs might be used for some purpose other than making a work of art. If you don't intend to take photographs, then strike out the request for permission to take them. If you do want photographs, then you may want to add a sentence clarifying how you intend to use them.

The third sentence addresses the one problem that may occur with people who pose in the nude and then become concerned that the exhibition or publication of your artwork would be an invasion of their privacy. Make sure you protect your prerogatives by including this sentence in any and every model release you prepare.

Paragraph ❷

This paragraph uses legal terminology to cover a host of potential problems. You may even want to expand it to make this agreement binding for all future modeling sessions so you won't have to get a signed agreement every time you hire the same model.

Having a Witness

By signing this document, the witness is certifying that both you and the model did, in fact, sign the document. That may seem like an unnecessary complication, but models have been known to be unpredictable individuals, so it's best to have this protection.

Date

MODEL RELEASE

❶ I hereby agree to pose as a model for _____ for a fee of $_____ per hour. I grant him/her permission to draw, paint, or otherwise record my image in any form or medium and to take photographs of me for the purposes of creating these works of art. Furthermore, I grant him/her permission to exhibit, publish, and or sell these works without any claims being made by me.

❷   I hereby warrant that I am of legal age, have the right to establish this agreement in my own name, and that these permissions are granted to _____, successors, legal representative, and assigns. Further, I warrant that I have read this model release agreement and agree to its contents.

_____   _____   _____   _____
SIGNATURE   DATE   WITNESS   DATE

_____   _____
ADDRESS   ADDRESS

Invoice

HOW TO USE THIS LETTER

Many of the individuals and corporations with which you do business will pay their bills through an accountant or accounting department. In those situations, you will need to send a formal invoice for services rendered or items delivered in order to be paid. In other words, the accountant needs some paperwork prepared by you and approved by your client before a check can be issued.

Make sure you describe the product or service for which you want payment, itemizing any expenses, listing the numbers on any purchase orders you have received, and attaching copies of receipts for your expenses.

Under existing law, if the copyright is not specifically transferred, it is assumed that the copyright to the work being sold will remain with the artist. Accordingly, there is no need to mention copyright specifically. At times, however, in order to avoid any doubt or future problems, it is advisable to state that "reproduction rights are reserved to the artist," or that "reproduction rights are not included in the sale of this artwork."

Sign the original invoice and include either your corporate name (with your resale tax number) or your Social Security number. Finally, make a photocopy of your invoice and place it in your files.

Date

Name of Individual or Corporate Officer
Business Name
Street Address
City, State, Zip

Dear _____:

DESCRIPTION:

AMOUNT DUE $_____.____

Thank you,

Your Name
Your Social Security Number or Corporate Name
Street Address
City, State, Zip
Phone and/or Fax

The Letters of Agreement

HOW TO USE THESE FORMS

The letters that follow, on pages 35-127, are provided for you to use in your business dealings. Blanks are provided where you may fill in the information pertaining to the agreements you make with gallery owners, agents, publishers, and the like.

The letters have been perforated for convenient removal from the book. Still, we recommend that care be taken in tearing along the perforation, so that the chance of an unwanted rip along the edge is avoided.

These letters have been designed to be typed upon without any special adjustment of your typewriter carriage. In other words, no special effort should be needed to line up the blanks in the letter as you move from one line to the next; a simple use of the carriage return should suffice to provide a correct line-up and ample space for your machine's typeface.

Before you make use of any given letter, you should refer to the preceding explanation for the letter (see pages 6–33) and read it carefully. It will serve as a guide to the important points to which you should give consideration before and during discussions with the person who will receive the letter. The samples that are provided with the explanations sometimes show percentages and amounts in the blank spaces; these are intended simply as standards, to suggest numbers that are commonly agreed upon in dealings of this kind.

Obviously, we recommend that you fill in the blanks in the letter only *after* you have had a conversation with the intended recipient. In this conversation, you should reach the agreements on which your relationship will be based. The letter should serve to *reiterate and confirm* your agreement, not to initiate a discussion or to make your first proposals for a business relationship with that person.

If there are phrases or sentences that do not pertain to the agreement that arises from your conversation, you should strike out those passages. You may prefer, however, to rewrite the letter as your agreement dictates, following the language provided. You will find that these letters serve as excellent models for standard letters of agreement. A word of caution: Be sure you do not introduce loopholes into the wording of the letter.

You should, of course, fill in the date and the recipient's name and address at the top. Also fill in your name, address, phone and/or fax number at the bottom, and remember to add your signature.

If possible, as a courtesy you should enclose a photocopy of the letter, as filled in by you, for the recipient to sign and return, and a self-addressed envelope. Clearly, it's also a good idea to retain a photocopy for your own files as well.

Good luck!

Beginning a Business Relationship with a Group Exhibition

_____   _____
_____
_____
_____

Dear _____:

I am very pleased to have my artwork included in your upcoming group exhibition from _____ to _____. I hope that this will develop into a profitable relationship for both of us.

I thought it might be helpful to send you the enclosed information, which tells a little more about me and the works you will be displaying. Also, I am writing to summarize the arrangements we discussed informally. I trust you don't mind my putting this down in a letter and asking you to return a signed copy. Once I have received your signed copy, I will ship my works to your gallery. This bit of formality will help me feel that I have taken care of business matters and can concentrate on what I do best—my art!

The ___ works of mine that you have chosen for your exhibition are tagged on the back so that you can easily identify them. They are as follows:

1 Title, date, and dimensions: _____.
   We have agreed on a retail price of $_____ for this work.
2. Title, date, and dimensions:_____.
   We have agreed on a retail price of $_____ for this work.
3. Title, date, and dimensions:_____.
   We have agreed on a retail price of $_____ for this work.
4. Title, date, and dimensions:_____.
   We have agreed on a retail price of $_____ for this work.
5. Title, date, and dimensions:_____.
   We have agreed on a retail price of $_____ for this work.
6. Title, date, and dimensions:_____.
   We have agreed on a retail price of $_____ for this work.

We have also agreed that you will take a _____ percent commission on the sale of each of these works, payable within _____ days of the sale. Because you and I have not yet established a permanent business relationship, I must ask that you pay me a full _____ percent of the selling price, even if you do not receive full payment from a client who takes possession of my work. I understand that it is your practice to offer a ___ percent discount to a limited number of preferred clients, and I accept that this practice may result in my receiving proportionally less for my works.

For my inventory records, I would appreciate receiving the names and addresses of the persons or corporations that purchase my art, so that I might contact them in the future either to borrow the works back for an exhibition or to rephotograph them.

In the event that works do not sell by the closing dates of the exhibition, _____, I would appreciate your sending them back to me in the crates in which they were delivered. The expense of shipping and insuring the works that are returned to me will be paid by _____. The expense of _____ will be covered by _____.

I certainly hope the collectors who visit your gallery respond favorably to my art and that you will be interested in exhibiting my work again in the future. I would appreciate your keeping me in mind when you are organizing future theme shows or considering new choices for the gallery's regular roster of artists.

Assuming you are in agreement with what I have described in this letter, I would appreciate your signing the enclosed copy and returning it to me in the self-addressed envelope. If there are any points that need further discussion or clarification, please give me a call or drop me a note.

Again, I am glad to have my art displayed in your gallery as part of a terrific exhibition. Thank you for your interest in my work.

Sincerely yours,

ACKNOWLEDGED:

_____   _____
SIGNATURE   DATE
                                          _____
_____
TITLE   _____

_____   _____

_____

_____

_____

_____

Dear _____:

I am very pleased to have my artwork included in your upcoming group exhibition from _____ to _____. I hope that this will develop into a profitable relationship for both of us.

 I thought it might be helpful to send you the enclosed information, which tells a little more about me and the works you will be displaying. Also, I am writing to summarize the arrangements we discussed informally. I trust you don't mind my putting this down in a letter and asking you to return a signed copy. Once I have received your signed copy, I will ship my works to your gallery. This bit of formality will help me feel that I have taken care of business matters and can concentrate on what I do best—my art!

 The ___ works of mine that you have chosen for your exhibition are tagged on the back so that you can easily identify them. They are as follows:

  1 Title, date, and dimensions: _____.
  We have agreed on a retail price of $_____ for this work.
  2. Title, date, and dimensions:_____.
  We have agreed on a retail price of $_____ for this work.
  3. Title, date, and dimensions:_____.
  We have agreed on a retail price of $_____ for this work.
  4. Title, date, and dimensions:_____.
  We have agreed on a retail price of $_____ for this work.
  5. Title, date, and dimensions:_____.
  We have agreed on a retail price of $_____ for this work.
  6. Title, date, and dimensions:_____.
  We have agreed on a retail price of $_____ for this work.

We have also agreed that you will take a _____ percent commission on the sale of each of these works, payable within _____ days of the sale. Because you and I have not yet established a permanent business relationship, I must ask that you pay me a full _____ percent of the selling price, even if you do not receive full payment from a client who takes possession of my work. I understand that it is your practice to offer a ___ percent discount to a limited number of preferred clients, and I accept that this practice may result in my receiving proportionally less for my works.

 For my inventory records, I would appreciate receiving the names and addresses of the persons or corporations that purchase my art, so that I might contact them in the future either to borrow the works back for an exhibition or to rephotograph them.

 In the event that works do not sell by the closing dates of the exhibition, _____, I would appreciate your sending them back to me in the crates in which they were delivered. The expense of shipping and insuring the works that are returned to me will be paid by _____. The expense of _____ will be covered by _____.

 I certainly hope the collectors who visit your gallery respond favorably to my art and that you will be interested in exhibiting my work again in the future. I would appreciate your keeping me in mind when you are organizing future theme shows or considering new choices for the gallery's regular roster of artists.

 Assuming you are in agreement with what I have described in this letter, I would appreciate your signing the enclosed copy and returning it to me in the self-addressed envelope. If there are any points that need further discussion or clarification, please give me a call or drop me a note.

 Again, I am glad to have my art displayed in your gallery as part of a terrific exhibition. Thank you for your interest in my work.

Sincerely yours,

ACKNOWLEDGED:

_____   _____
SIGNATURE   DATE

_____   _____
TITLE   _____

_____

_____
_____
_____
_____

Dear _____:

I am very pleased to have my artwork included in your upcoming group exhibition from _____ to _____. I hope that this will develop into a profitable relationship for both of us.

    I thought it might be helpful to send you the enclosed information, which tells a little more about me and the works you will be displaying. Also, I am writing to summarize the arrangements we discussed informally. I trust you don't mind my putting this down in a letter and asking you to return a signed copy. Once I have received your signed copy, I will ship my works to your gallery. This bit of formality will help me feel that I have taken care of business matters and can concentrate on what I do best—my art!

    The ___ works of mine that you have chosen for your exhibition are tagged on the back so that you can easily identify them. They are as follows:

      1 Title, date, and dimensions: _____.
      We have agreed on a retail price of $_____ for this work.
      2. Title, date, and dimensions:_____.
      We have agreed on a retail price of $_____ for this work.
      3. Title, date, and dimensions:_____.
      We have agreed on a retail price of $_____ for this work.
      4. Title, date, and dimensions:_____.
      We have agreed on a retail price of $_____ for this work.
      5. Title, date, and dimensions:_____.
      We have agreed on a retail price of $_____ for this work.
      6. Title, date, and dimensions:_____.
      We have agreed on a retail price of $_____ for this work.

    We have also agreed that you will take a _____ percent commission on the sale of each of these works, payable within _____ days of the sale. Because you and I have not yet established a permanent business relationship, I must ask that you pay me a full _____ percent of the selling price, even if you do not receive full payment from a client who takes possession of my work. I understand that it is your practice to offer a ___ percent discount to a limited number of preferred clients, and I accept that this practice may result in my receiving proportionally less for my works.

    For my inventory records, I would appreciate receiving the names and addresses of the persons or corporations that purchase my art, so that I might contact them in the future either to borrow the works back for an exhibition or to rephotograph them.

    In the event that works do not sell by the closing dates of the exhibition, _____, I would appreciate your sending them back to me in the crates in which they were delivered. The expense of shipping and insuring the works that are returned to me will be paid by _____. The expense of _____ will be covered by _____.

    I certainly hope the collectors who visit your gallery respond favorably to my art and that you will be interested in exhibiting my work again in the future. I would appreciate your keeping me in mind when you are organizing future theme shows or considering new choices for the gallery's regular roster of artists.

    Assuming you are in agreement with what I have described in this letter, I would appreciate your signing the enclosed copy and returning it to me in the self-addressed envelope. If there are any points that need further discussion or clarification, please give me a call or drop me a note.

    Again, I am glad to have my art displayed in your gallery as part of a terrific exhibition. Thank you for your interest in my work.

                               Sincerely yours,

ACKNOWLEDGED:

_____   _____
SIGNATURE   DATE   _____

TITLE   _____

_____

_____
_____
_____
_____

Dear _____:

I am very pleased to have my artwork included in your upcoming group exhibition from _____ to _____. I hope that this will develop into a profitable relationship for both of us.

I thought it might be helpful to send you the enclosed information, which tells a little more about me and the works you will be displaying. Also, I am writing to summarize the arrangements we discussed informally. I trust you don't mind my putting this down in a letter and asking you to return a signed copy. Once I have received your signed copy, I will ship my works to your gallery. This bit of formality will help me feel that I have taken care of business matters and can concentrate on what I do best—my art!

The ___ works of mine that you have chosen for your exhibition are tagged on the back so that you can easily identify them. They are as follows:

1 Title, date, and dimensions: _____.
   We have agreed on a retail price of $_____ for this work.
2. Title, date, and dimensions:_____.
   We have agreed on a retail price of $_____ for this work.
3. Title, date, and dimensions:_____.
   We have agreed on a retail price of $_____ for this work.
4. Title, date, and dimensions:_____.
   We have agreed on a retail price of $_____ for this work.
5. Title, date, and dimensions:_____.
   We have agreed on a retail price of $_____ for this work.
6. Title, date, and dimensions:_____.
   We have agreed on a retail price of $_____ for this work.

We have also agreed that you will take a _____ percent commission on the sale of each of these works, payable within _____ days of the sale. Because you and I have not yet established a permanent business relationship, I must ask that you pay me a full _____ percent of the selling price, even if you do not receive full payment from a client who takes possession of my work. I understand that it is your practice to offer a ___ percent discount to a limited number of preferred clients, and I accept that this practice may result in my receiving proportionally less for my works.

For my inventory records, I would appreciate receiving the names and addresses of the persons or corporations that purchase my art, so that I might contact them in the future either to borrow the works back for an exhibition or to rephotograph them.

In the event that works do not sell by the closing dates of the exhibition, _____, I would appreciate your sending them back to me in the crates in which they were delivered. The expense of shipping and insuring the works that are returned to me will be paid by _____. The expense of _____ will be covered by _____.

I certainly hope the collectors who visit your gallery respond favorably to my art and that you will be interested in exhibiting my work again in the future. I would appreciate your keeping me in mind when you are organizing future theme shows or considering new choices for the gallery's regular roster of artists.

Assuming you are in agreement with what I have described in this letter, I would appreciate your signing the enclosed copy and returning it to me in the self-addressed envelope. If there are any points that need further discussion or clarification, please give me a call or drop me a note.

Again, I am glad to have my art displayed in your gallery as part of a terrific exhibition. Thank you for your interest in my work.

Sincerely yours,

ACKNOWLEDGED:

_____   _____

_____   _____
SIGNATURE   DATE

_____   _____
TITLE

Sending Prints or Reproductions to Galleries

———————————————————————

———————————————————
———————————————————
———————————————————
———————————————————

Dear _____:

Thank you for the interest you expressed recently regarding limited editions of my work. I would very much like to sell these through your gallery, and I hope that this will be the start of a profitable relationship between us.

I am writing to review some of the topics we discussed, just to be sure that I clearly understand how we will be working together. If my recollection is in any way inaccurate, please let me know immediately. If, on the other hand, you agree with the points covered in this letter, I would appreciate your signing the enclosed copy and returning it to me for my records.

You have asked me to send you _____ copies each of _____ limited-edition works. Specifically, you are interested in the works listed here:

Title_____ (____ × _____", retail price $_____)
Other features: _____
Title_____ (____ × _____", retail price $_____)
Other features: _____
Title_____ (____ × _____", retail price $_____)
Other features: _____
Title_____ (____ × _____", retail price $_____)
Other features: _____
Title_____ (____ × _____", retail price $_____)
Other features: _____
Title_____ (____ × _____", retail price $_____)
Other features: _____

I will be glad to cover the cost of packing, insuring, and shipping these works to your gallery.

We have agreed that you will take a _____ percent commission on the sale of these prints/reproductions, with the balance due me within _____ days of any sale. The retail prices may not be discounted, and I will expect to receive my _____ percent of the purchase price within _____ days after a client takes possession of a work, even if the client has not paid in full.

In the event that one or more of these works does not sell within _____ months of your receipt of the work, I will expect you either to return the unsold items or to purchase them from me at _____ percent of the retail price.

Please review the biographical materials that I have included, which I hope will be helpful to you. I do ask that you return the _____ to me in good condition.

Again, I'm very pleased to have these limited editions of my work made available through your gallery. I hope they sell quickly and that you and I can discuss making more of my work available to your clients. Please let me know if you have any questions or concerns.

Sincerely yours,

ACKNOWLEDGED: ———————————————————

                                                 ———————————————————
———————————————————————   ———————————————————
SIGNATURE   DATE   ———————————————————

———————————————————————
TITLE

_____

_____
_____
_____
_____

Dear _____:

Thank you for the interest you expressed recently regarding limited editions of my work. I would very much like to sell these through your gallery, and I hope that this will be the start of a profitable relationship between us.

I am writing to review some of the topics we discussed, just to be sure that I clearly understand how we will be working together. If my recollection is in any way inaccurate, please let me know immediately. If, on the other hand, you agree with the points covered in this letter, I would appreciate your signing the enclosed copy and returning it to me for my records.

You have asked me to send you _____ copies each of _____ limited-edition works. Specifically, you are interested in the works listed here:

Title_____ (___ × _____", retail price $_____)
Other features: _____
Title_____ (___ × _____", retail price $_____)
Other features: _____
Title_____ (___ × _____", retail price $_____)
Other features: _____
Title_____ (___ × _____", retail price $_____)
Other features: _____
Title_____ (___ × _____", retail price $_____)
Other features: _____
Title_____ (___ × _____", retail price $_____)
Other features: _____

I will be glad to cover the cost of packing, insuring, and shipping these works to your gallery.

We have agreed that you will take a _____ percent commission on the sale of these prints/reproductions, with the balance due me within _____ days of any sale. The retail prices may not be discounted, and I will expect to receive my _____ percent of the purchase price within _____ days after a client takes possession of a work, even if the client has not paid in full.

In the event that one or more of these works does not sell within _____ months of your receipt of the work, I will expect you either to return the unsold items or to purchase them from me at _____ percent of the retail price.

Please review the biographical materials that I have included, which I hope will be helpful to you. I do ask that you return the _____ to me in good condition.

Again, I'm very pleased to have these limited editions of my work made available through your gallery. I hope they sell quickly and that you and I can discuss making more of my work available to your clients. Please let me know if you have any questions or concerns.

Sincerely yours,

ACKNOWLEDGED: _____

_____   _____
SIGNATURE   DATE   _____

_____
TITLE

_____

_____
_____
_____
_____

Dear _____:

Thank you for the interest you expressed recently regarding limited editions of my work. I would very much like to sell these through your gallery, and I hope that this will be the start of a profitable relationship between us.

I am writing to review some of the topics we discussed, just to be sure that I clearly understand how we will be working together. If my recollection is in any way inaccurate, please let me know immediately. If, on the other hand, you agree with the points covered in this letter, I would appreciate your signing the enclosed copy and returning it to me for my records.

You have asked me to send you _____ copies each of _____ limited-edition works. Specifically, you are interested in the works listed here:

Title_____ (____ × _____", retail price $_____)
Other features: _____
Title_____ (____ × _____", retail price $_____)
Other features: _____
Title_____ (____ × _____", retail price $_____)
Other features: _____
Title_____ (____ × _____", retail price $_____)
Other features: _____
Title_____ (____ × _____", retail price $_____)
Other features: _____
Title_____ (____ × _____", retail price $_____)
Other features: _____

I will be glad to cover the cost of packing, insuring, and shipping these works to your gallery.

We have agreed that you will take a _____ percent commission on the sale of these prints/reproductions, with the balance due me within _____ days of any sale. The retail prices may not be discounted, and I will expect to receive my _____ percent of the purchase price within _____ days after a client takes possession of a work, even if the client has not paid in full.

In the event that one or more of these works does not sell within _____ months of your receipt of the work, I will expect you either to return the unsold items or to purchase them from me at _____ percent of the retail price.

Please review the biographical materials that I have included, which I hope will be helpful to you. I do ask that you return the _____ to me in good condition.

Again, I'm very pleased to have these limited editions of my work made available through your gallery. I hope they sell quickly and that you and I can discuss making more of my work available to your clients. Please let me know if you have any questions or concerns.

Sincerely yours,

ACKNOWLEDGED: _____

_____   _____
SIGNATURE   DATE   _____

_____
TITLE

Sending Prints or Reproductions to Galleries

_____

_____
_____
_____
_____

Dear _____:

Thank you for the interest you expressed recently regarding limited editions of my work. I would very much like to sell these through your gallery, and I hope that this will be the start of a profitable relationship between us.

I am writing to review some of the topics we discussed, just to be sure that I clearly understand how we will be working together. If my recollection is in any way inaccurate, please let me know immediately. If, on the other hand, you agree with the points covered in this letter, I would appreciate your signing the enclosed copy and returning it to me for my records.

You have asked me to send you _____ copies each of _____ limited-edition works. Specifically, you are interested in the works listed here:

Title_____ (____ × _____", retail price $_____)
Other features: _____
Title_____ (____ × _____", retail price $_____)
Other features: _____
Title_____ (____ × _____", retail price $_____)
Other features: _____
Title_____ (____ × _____", retail price $_____)
Other features: _____
Title_____ (____ × _____", retail price $_____)
Other features: _____
Title_____ (____ × _____", retail price $_____)
Other features: _____

I will be glad to cover the cost of packing, insuring, and shipping these works to your gallery.

We have agreed that you will take a _____ percent commission on the sale of these prints/reproductions, with the balance due me within _____ days of any sale. The retail prices may not be discounted, and I will expect to receive my _____ percent of the purchase price within _____ days after a client takes possession of a work, even if the client has not paid in full.

In the event that one or more of these works does not sell within _____ months of your receipt of the work, I will expect you either to return the unsold items or to purchase them from me at _____ percent of the retail price.

Please review the biographical materials that I have included, which I hope will be helpful to you. I do ask that you return the _____ to me in good condition.

Again, I'm very pleased to have these limited editions of my work made available through your gallery. I hope they sell quickly and that you and I can discuss making more of my work available to your clients. Please let me know if you have any questions or concerns.

Sincerely yours,

ACKNOWLEDGED: _____
                                                        _____
_____   _____
SIGNATURE   DATE
                                                        _____
_____
TITLE

_____

_____
_____
_____
_____

Dear _____:

I am delighted to have the opportunity to exhibit my artwork in your space and, again, I thank you for making this display possible. You are performing a great service to me and, I hope, to the people of the community who see my works as a result.

I want to confirm the dates and arrangements we discussed so that I am clear about both my obligations and the services being provided by you. If any of the points I cover in this letter are not completely accurate, or if you would prefer that someone else associated with the space review this agreement, I would appreciate your letting me know right away. Otherwise, I would ask that you please sign the enclosed copy of this letter and return it to me for my records.

You have kindly made available the dates of _____ through _____, 19____, for the exhibition of my artwork. The exact number and placement of works will be determined when I deliver and install them on _____.

Knowing that the employees working near the exhibition will be busy with their responsibilities, I will provide signs and information for customers and will handle inquiries and sales by myself. The information will include some biographical facts, my address and phone number, and the titles, dates, dimensions, and prices of the artwork. It's my understanding that you are not expecting any payment for the use of the space or a commission on any sales that take place as a result of the exhibition.

I understand that you will / will not insure my artworks while on display. I would appreciate every effort being made to protect them from damage or theft. For my own insurance purposes, I may want to photograph the works while they are on display in your space. I will notify you of other access that I may need, to show or sell my work.

I will also make arrangements to remove the artworks after the last day of the exhibition, and I will take away any signs and remaining copies of the information I provided.

Again, thank you for giving me this opportunity to exhibit my artwork.

Sincerely yours,

_____
_____
_____
_____

ACKNOWLEDGED:

_____
SIGNATURE   DATE

_____
TITLE

Agreeing to Exhibit in a Business Establishment: Banks, Restaurants, Office Lobbies, etc.

_____

_____
_____
_____
_____

Dear _____:

I am delighted to have the opportunity to exhibit my artwork in your space and, again, I thank you for making this display possible. You are performing a great service to me and, I hope, to the people of the community who see my works as a result.

I want to confirm the dates and arrangements we discussed so that I am clear about both my obligations and the services being provided by you. If any of the points I cover in this letter are not completely accurate, or if you would prefer that someone else associated with the space review this agreement, I would appreciate your letting me know right away. Otherwise, I would ask that you please sign the enclosed copy of this letter and return it to me for my records.

You have kindly made available the dates of _____ through _____, 19____, for the exhibition of my artwork. The exact number and placement of works will be determined when I deliver and install them on _____.

Knowing that the employees working near the exhibition will be busy with their responsibilities, I will provide signs and information for customers and will handle inquiries and sales by myself. The information will include some biographical facts, my address and phone number, and the titles, dates, dimensions, and prices of the artwork. It's my understanding that you are not expecting any payment for the use of the space or a commission on any sales that take place as a result of the exhibition.

I understand that you will / will not insure my artworks while on display. I would appreciate every effort being made to protect them from damage or theft. For my own insurance purposes, I may want to photograph the works while they are on display in your space. I will notify you of other access that I may need, to show or sell my work.

I will also make arrangements to remove the artworks after the last day of the exhibition, and I will take away any signs and remaining copies of the information I provided.

Again, thank you for giving me this opportunity to exhibit my artwork.

Sincerely yours,

_____
_____
_____
_____

ACKNOWLEDGED:

_____   _____
SIGNATURE   DATE

_____
TITLE

_____

_____
_____
_____
_____

Dear _____ :

I am delighted to have the opportunity to exhibit my artwork in your space and, again, I thank you for making this display possible. You are performing a great service to me and, I hope, to the people of the community who see my works as a result.

I want to confirm the dates and arrangements we discussed so that I am clear about both my obligations and the services being provided by you. If any of the points I cover in this letter are not completely accurate, or if you would prefer that someone else associated with the space review this agreement, I would appreciate your letting me know right away. Otherwise, I would ask that you please sign the enclosed copy of this letter and return it to me for my records.

You have kindly made available the dates of _____ through _____, 19____, for the exhibition of my artwork. The exact number and placement of works will be determined when I deliver and install them on _____.

Knowing that the employees working near the exhibition will be busy with their responsibilities, I will provide signs and information for customers and will handle inquiries and sales by myself. The information will include some biographical facts, my address and phone number, and the titles, dates, dimensions, and prices of the artwork. It's my understanding that you are not expecting any payment for the use of the space or a commission on any sales that take place as a result of the exhibition.

I understand that you will / will not insure my artworks while on display. I would appreciate every effort being made to protect them from damage or theft. For my own insurance purposes, I may want to photograph the works while they are on display in your space. I will notify you of other access that I may need, to show or sell my work.

I will also make arrangements to remove the artworks after the last day of the exhibition, and I will take away any signs and remaining copies of the information I provided.

Again, thank you for giving me this opportunity to exhibit my artwork.

Sincerely yours,

_____
_____
_____
_____

ACKNOWLEDGED:

_____
SIGNATURE   DATE

_____
TITLE

_____

_____
_____
_____
_____
_____

Dear _____:

I am very pleased to have talked to you about showing my artwork in your gallery. I look forward to working with you and your staff and hope this will become a very profitable relationship for everyone.

Just so I am clear about the various matters we discussed, I will briefly review our discussion here. If my recollections are not completely accurate, I would appreciate your letting me know. Otherwise, please sign a copy of this letter and return it to me at your earliest convenience.

As you know, I have enjoyed a supportive relationship with dealers in other parts of the country. I want to maintain those business associations while taking advantage of the opportunity you are offering. For that reason, I want to make it clear that the agreement between us is not exclusive and that I will be free to exhibit and sell my work through galleries in other cities.

Art collectors do buy from dealers located in different cities, and galleries often sell to clients outside their geographic locations, but to the extent possible, I will not offer my artwork through other galleries or agents who actively sell artwork in your area on a regular basis. I will not sell directly to any individuals or corporations based in your city but will refer those prospective clients to you.

We discussed your including several of my artworks in group shows and then, perhaps, presenting a solo exhibition of my work, and we decided _____ _____. I am happy with that arrangement and will send you the works we discussed. I will crate, ship, and insure them at _____ expense and will forward an inventory list of the titles, dates, dimensions, and retail prices for your records. If there is any problem with this shipment, I would appreciate your letting me know immediately.

We have agreed that you will take a _____ percent commission on the sale of any of my works, and that the balance will be due to me within _____ days of the sale. While I recognize that you may wish to extend discounts and/or a schedule of payment terms to your clients, I do ask that you pay my _____ percent of the retail price of any sold artwork within _____ days of the date when a client takes possession of it.

I think it would be best for us to establish a time frame for our business agreement. I suggest that we reevaluate our agreement after _____ to determine whether it has been mutually beneficial and is worth continuing. Unless you have objections, I will assume that our agreement will be in effect for _____ from the date of this letter.

Sincerely yours,

ACKNOWLEDGED: _____
                                                 _____
_____   _____
SIGNATURE   DATE   _____

_____
TITLE

_____

_____
_____
_____
_____
_____

Dear _____:

I am very pleased to have talked to you about showing my artwork in your gallery. I look forward to working with you and your staff and hope this will become a very profitable relationship for everyone.

Just so I am clear about the various matters we discussed, I will briefly review our discussion here. If my recollections are not completely accurate, I would appreciate your letting me know. Otherwise, please sign a copy of this letter and return it to me at your earliest convenience.

As you know, I have enjoyed a supportive relationship with dealers in other parts of the country. I want to maintain those business associations while taking advantage of the opportunity you are offering. For that reason, I want to make it clear that the agreement between us is not exclusive and that I will be free to exhibit and sell my work through galleries in other cities.

Art collectors do buy from dealers located in different cities, and galleries often sell to clients outside their geographic locations, but to the extent possible, I will not offer my artwork through other galleries or agents who actively sell artwork in your area on a regular basis. I will not sell directly to any individuals or corporations based in your city but will refer those prospective clients to you.

We discussed your including several of my artworks in group shows and then, perhaps, presenting a solo exhibition of my work, and we decided _____ _____. I am happy with that arrangement and will send you the works we discussed. I will crate, ship, and insure them at _____ expense and will forward an inventory list of the titles, dates, dimensions, and retail prices for your records. If there is any problem with this shipment, I would appreciate your letting me know immediately.

We have agreed that you will take a _____ percent commission on the sale of any of my works, and that the balance will be due to me within _____ days of the sale. While I recognize that you may wish to extend discounts and/or a schedule of payment terms to your clients, I do ask that you pay my _____ percent of the retail price of any sold artwork within _____ days of the date when a client takes possession of it.

I think it would be best for us to establish a time frame for our business agreement. I suggest that we reevaluate our agreement after _____ to determine whether it has been mutually beneficial and is worth continuing. Unless you have objections, I will assume that our agreement will be in effect for _____ from the date of this letter.

Sincerely yours,

ACKNOWLEDGED: _____

_____   _____
SIGNATURE   DATE

_____
TITLE

Confirming Gallery Representation Within a Limited Geographic Area

_____

_____
_____
_____
_____
_____

Dear _____ :

I am very pleased to have talked to you about showing my artwork in your gallery. I look forward to working with you and your staff and hope this will become a very profitable relationship for everyone.

Just so I am clear about the various matters we discussed, I will briefly review our discussion here. If my recollections are not completely accurate, I would appreciate your letting me know. Otherwise, please sign a copy of this letter and return it to me at your earliest convenience.

As you know, I have enjoyed a supportive relationship with dealers in other parts of the country. I want to maintain those business associations while taking advantage of the opportunity you are offering. For that reason, I want to make it clear that the agreement between us is not exclusive and that I will be free to exhibit and sell my work through galleries in other cities.

Art collectors do buy from dealers located in different cities, and galleries often sell to clients outside their geographic locations, but to the extent possible, I will not offer my artwork through other galleries or agents who actively sell artwork in your area on a regular basis. I will not sell directly to any individuals or corporations based in your city but will refer those prospective clients to you.

We discussed your including several of my artworks in group shows and then, perhaps, presenting a solo exhibition of my work, and we decided _____
_____. I am happy with that arrangement and will send you the works we discussed. I will crate, ship, and insure them at _____ expense and will forward an inventory list of the titles, dates, dimensions, and retail prices for your records. If there is any problem with this shipment, I would appreciate your letting me know immediately.

We have agreed that you will take a _____ percent commission on the sale of any of my works, and that the balance will be due to me within _____ days of the sale. While I recognize that you may wish to extend discounts and/or a schedule of payment terms to your clients, I do ask that you pay my _____ percent of the retail price of any sold artwork within _____ days of the date when a client takes possession of it.

I think it would be best for us to establish a time frame for our business agreement. I suggest that we reevaluate our agreement after _____ to determine whether it has been mutually beneficial and is worth continuing. Unless you have objections, I will assume that our agreement will be in effect for _____ from the date of this letter.

Sincerely yours,

ACKNOWLEDGED:

_____

_____   _____
SIGNATURE   DATE   _____

_____   _____
TITLE

_____

_____
_____
_____
_____

Dear _____:

I have given a good deal of thought to the matters we recently discussed, and I am writing to review the main points of our discussion in this letter. Before I do that, however, I must say again that I am very pleased I am to be offered exclusive representation by your gallery. It is an opportunity that will be, I hope, profitable for both of us for years to come. The arrangement does call for each of us to make commitments to the other, and I want to clarify those as we establish a formal agreement.

    The retail price of my artwork will be established by mutual consent, and the gallery will receive a _____ percent commission on the sale of any and all artwork that I have created or will create for as long as our agreement is in effect. This will include sales by you only/sales by me, and sales to my existing clients, as well as those who purchase my work through your gallery. We have agreed that you will not be due a commission on any artwork that I give free of charge to family members, charitable organizations, or public institutions, even if these are subsequently sold by the recipient. Furthermore, you will not have any claim on works created during the period our agreement is in effect that are not sold during that same period.

    We have agreed that I will receive _____ percent of the retail price for any of my artwork sold while our agreement is in effect, payable within _____ days of your receiving all or part of the total retail price. In the event that a client makes partial payment, you will send me _____ percent of the monies received within _____ days until such time as the full amount is paid.

    Knowing that it is customary for you to offer a _____ percent discount to preferred customers, I agree that in those situations I will be paid my standard _____ percent on the discounted retail price. Any further discounts will be absorbed by your gallery. If the artwork is sold through another gallery or agent, you will split the dealer's commission, and I will receive _____ percent of the retail selling price. No matter how my artwork is sold, I will receive the names and addresses of the individuals, corporations, or institutions purchasing that work.

    It will be my responsibility to create the artwork, deliver it to the gallery, and pay all the expenses related to those activities. Additionally, I agree to do the following:_____
_____.

The gallery will be responsible for presenting, insuring, and promoting the sale of that artwork and handling the related business matters. The gallery will pay the expenses associated with those activities, including the cost of advertising the exhibitions, mailing exhibition announcements, and providing refreshments at openings. Additionally, the gallery agrees to do the following: _____
_____.

    Like any other artist, I am eager for my artwork to be seen by as many people as possible, and I want to be sure that I have opportunities to present a solo exhibition at least once every _____ year(s) and to participate in group exhibitions at least once every _____. I will expect the gallery to exhibit my artwork with that kind of frequency and make it available for viewing by prospective clients at all times.

    I suggest that we consider our agreement in effect for a period of _____ and that we review the progress of our relationship every _____. I will assume that is agreeable to you unless you suggest another time frame.

    I believe that covers the most important points relating to our proposed business relationship. If I have forgotten anything, or if I have not outlined the agreement as you believe it should exist, I would appreciate your letting me know as soon as possible. If, on the other hand, you are in agreement with me on these matters, please sign the enclosed copy and return it to me at your earliest convenience.

Sincerely yours,

ACKNOWLEDGED:

_____

_____

_____
NAME   DATE

_____
TITLE

_____

_____
_____
_____
_____

Dear _____:

I have given a good deal of thought to the matters we recently discussed, and I am writing to review the main points of our discussion in this letter. Before I do that, however, I must say again that I am very pleased I am to be offered exclusive representation by your gallery. It is an opportunity that will be, I hope, profitable for both of us for years to come. The arrangement does call for each of us to make commitments to the other, and I want to clarify those as we establish a formal agreement.

The retail price of my artwork will be established by mutual consent, and the gallery will receive a _____ percent commission on the sale of any and all artwork that I have created or will create for as long as our agreement is in effect. This will include sales by you only/sales by me, and sales to my existing clients, as well as those who purchase my work through your gallery. We have agreed that you will not be due a commission on any artwork that I give free of charge to family members, charitable organizations, or public institutions, even if these are subsequently sold by the recipient. Furthermore, you will not have any claim on works created during the period our agreement is in effect that are not sold during that same period.

We have agreed that I will receive _____ percent of the retail price for any of my artwork sold while our agreement is in effect, payable within _____ days of your receiving all or part of the total retail price. In the event that a client makes partial payment, you will send me _____ percent of the monies received within _____days until such time as the full amount is paid.

Knowing that it is customary for you to offer a _____ percent discount to preferred customers, I agree that in those situations I will be paid my standard _____ percent on the discounted retail price. Any further discounts will be absorbed by your gallery. If the artwork is sold through another gallery or agent, you will split the dealer's commission, and I will receive _____ percent of the retail selling price. No matter how my artwork is sold, I will receive the names and addresses of the individuals, corporations, or institutions purchasing that work.

It will be my responsibility to create the artwork, deliver it to the gallery, and pay all the expenses related to those activities. Additionally, I agree to do the following:_____
_____.

The gallery will be responsible for presenting, insuring, and promoting the sale of that artwork and handling the related business matters. The gallery will pay the expenses associated with those activities, including the cost of advertising the exhibitions, mailing exhibition announcements, and providing refreshments at openings. Additionally, the gallery agrees to do the following: _____
_____.

Like any other artist, I am eager for my artwork to be seen by as many people as possible, and I want to be sure that I have opportunities to present a solo exhibition at least once every ___ year(s) and to participate in group exhibitions at least once every _____. I will expect the gallery to exhibit my artwork with that kind of frequency and make it available for viewing by prospective clients at all times.

I suggest that we consider our agreement in effect for a period of _____ and that we review the progress of our relationship every _____. I will assume that is agreeable to you unless you suggest another time frame.

I believe that covers the most important points relating to our proposed business relationship. If I have forgotten anything, or if I have not outlined the agreement as you believe it should exist, I would appreciate your letting me know as soon as possible. If, on the other hand, you are in agreement with me on these matters, please sign the enclosed copy and return it to me at your earliest convenience.

Sincerely yours,

ACKNOWLEDGED: _____
                                                   _____
_____   _____
NAME   DATE   _____

_____
TITLE

_____

_____
_____
_____
_____

Dear _____:

I have given a good deal of thought to the matters we recently discussed, and I am writing to review the main points of our discussion in this letter. Before I do that, however, I must say again that I am very pleased I am to be offered exclusive representation by your gallery. It is an opportunity that will be, I hope, profitable for both of us for years to come. The arrangement does call for each of us to make commitments to the other, and I want to clarify those as we establish a formal agreement.

The retail price of my artwork will be established by mutual consent, and the gallery will receive a _____ percent commission on the sale of any and all artwork that I have created or will create for as long as our agreement is in effect. This will include sales by you only/sales by me, and sales to my existing clients, as well as those who purchase my work through your gallery. We have agreed that you will not be due a commission on any artwork that I give free of charge to family members, charitable organizations, or public institutions, even if these are subsequently sold by the recipient. Furthermore, you will not have any claim on works created during the period our agreement is in effect that are not sold during that same period.

We have agreed that I will receive _____ percent of the retail price for any of my artwork sold while our agreement is in effect, payable within _____ days of your receiving all or part of the total retail price. In the event that a client makes partial payment, you will send me _____ percent of the monies received within _____days until such time as the full amount is paid.

Knowing that it is customary for you to offer a _____ percent discount to preferred customers, I agree that in those situations I will be paid my standard _____ percent on the discounted retail price. Any further discounts will be absorbed by your gallery. If the artwork is sold through another gallery or agent, you will split the dealer's commission, and I will receive _____ percent of the retail selling price. No matter how my artwork is sold, I will receive the names and addresses of the individuals, corporations, or institutions purchasing that work.

It will be my responsibility to create the artwork, deliver it to the gallery, and pay all the expenses related to those activities. Additionally, I agree to do the following:_____
_____.

The gallery will be responsible for presenting, insuring, and promoting the sale of that artwork and handling the related business matters. The gallery will pay the expenses associated with those activities, including the cost of advertising the exhibitions, mailing exhibition announcements, and providing refreshments at openings. Additionally, the gallery agrees to do the following: _____
_____.

Like any other artist, I am eager for my artwork to be seen by as many people as possible, and I want to be sure that I have opportunities to present a solo exhibition at least once every ___ year(s) and to participate in group exhibitions at least once every _____. I will expect the gallery to exhibit my artwork with that kind of frequency and make it available for viewing by prospective clients at all times.

I suggest that we consider our agreement in effect for a period of _____ and that we review the progress of our relationship every _____. I will assume that is agreeable to you unless you suggest another time frame.

I believe that covers the most important points relating to our proposed business relationship. If I have forgotten anything, or if I have not outlined the agreement as you believe it should exist, I would appreciate your letting me know as soon as possible. If, on the other hand, you are in agreement with me on these matters, please sign the enclosed copy and return it to me at your earliest convenience.

Sincerely yours,

ACKNOWLEDGED: _____
                                                 _____
_____   _____   _____
NAME   DATE   _____

TITLE

_____

_____
_____
_____
_____
_____

Dear _____:

This letter is a follow-up to the conversation we recently had regarding your interest in publishing my artwork in your forthcoming _____.
I am delighted to have my work become a part of this publication, and I thank you for the request.

    I am enclosing _____ accurate photographs of the works you expressed interest in, each marked as to the title, date, dimensions, ownership, and gallery credit. These are professionally made photographs with color bars included next to the art, and they should allow you to get an accurate reproduction. If you have any questions about that accuracy, I would be happy to look over color proofs of the separations and indicate any color corrections that might improve the presentation.

    I have two important requests to make. The first is that you publish a caption with any reproduction of my artwork indicating that I own the copyright to the images. If you put the words "Copyright © 19___ by _____ _____" as close to the reproduction as possible, that will be fine. My second request is that you return the photographs to me as soon as you have finished using them. They are quite valuable, as you know, and I need to have them returned.

    I would very much like to have copies of your publication to share with friends and collectors, and I would appreciate your sending me _____ copies free of charge. I would also like to know how I might purchase additional discounted copies if I should need them in the future.

    If there is anything else you need for this project that I can help you with, please don't hesitate to get in touch with me. Again, many thanks for your interest in my work.

Sincerely yours,

_____
_____
_____
_____

ACKNOWLEDGED:

_____   _____
NAME   DATE

_____
TITLE

_____

_____
_____
_____
_____
_____

Dear _____:

This letter is a follow-up to the conversation we recently had regarding your
interest in publishing my artwork in your forthcoming _____.
I am delighted to have my work become a part of this publication, and I thank you
for the request.

I am enclosing _____ accurate photographs of the works you expressed
interest in, each marked as to the title, date, dimensions, ownership, and gallery
credit. These are professionally made photographs with color bars included next
to the art, and they should allow you to get an accurate reproduction. If you have
any questions about that accuracy, I would be happy to look over color proofs
of the separations and indicate any color corrections that might improve the
presentation.

I have two important requests to make. The first is that you publish a caption
with any reproduction of my artwork indicating that I own the copyright to the
images. If you put the words "Copyright © 19___ by _____
_____" as close to the reproduction as possible, that will be fine.
My second request is that you return the photographs to me as soon as you have
finished using them. They are quite valuable, as you know, and I need to have
them returned.

I would very much like to have copies of your publication to share with
friends and collectors, and I would appreciate your sending me _____ copies free
of charge. I would also like to know how I might purchase additional discounted
copies if I should need them in the future.

If there is anything else you need for this project that I can help you with,
please don't hesitate to get in touch with me. Again, many thanks for your interest
in my work.

Sincerely yours,

_____
_____
_____
_____

ACKNOWLEDGED:

_____
NAME   DATE
_____
TITLE

_____

_____
_____
_____
_____
_____

Dear _____:

This letter is a follow-up to the conversation we recently had regarding your
interest in publishing my artwork in your forthcoming _____.
I am delighted to have my work become a part of this publication, and I thank you
for the request.

    I am enclosing _____ accurate photographs of the works you expressed
interest in, each marked as to the title, date, dimensions, ownership, and gallery
credit. These are professionally made photographs with color bars included next
to the art, and they should allow you to get an accurate reproduction. If you have
any questions about that accuracy, I would be happy to look over color proofs
of the separations and indicate any color corrections that might improve the
presentation.

    I have two important requests to make. The first is that you publish a caption
with any reproduction of my artwork indicating that I own the copyright to the
images. If you put the words "Copyright © 19___ by _____
_____" as close to the reproduction as possible, that will be fine.
My second request is that you return the photographs to me as soon as you have
finished using them. They are quite valuable, as you know, and I need to have
them returned.

    I would very much like to have copies of your publication to share with
friends and collectors, and I would appreciate your sending me _____ copies free
of charge. I would also like to know how I might purchase additional discounted
copies if I should need them in the future.

    If there is anything else you need for this project that I can help you with,
please don't hesitate to get in touch with me. Again, many thanks for your interest
in my work.

Sincerely yours,

_____
_____
_____
_____

ACKNOWLEDGED:

_____
NAME   DATE

_____
TITLE

Allowing Publication of Reproductions Solely for Promotional Value

_____

_____
_____
_____
_____
_____

Dear _____:

This letter is a follow-up to our recent conversation regarding your interest in publishing a reproduction of my artwork entitled _____
_____. I am very pleased that you want to reproduce my work in this manner, and I only want to clarify a few points regarding this.

    As I explained, my principal concern is the quality of the reproduction. For that reason, I will only grant permission to use my artwork so long as I have the right to approve the selection of printing paper and the proofs of the color separations. Furthermore, while I don't wish to make things difficult for you, I would like to be able to approve the printer's color proofs.

    Under those conditions, I hereby agree to give your company, _____
_____, the right to print _____
copies of my artwork on _____" × _____" sheets. Each of these prints will include my name, the title of the artwork, and the words "Copyright © 19___ by _____." No other use may be made of this or any other of my copyrighted artwork without my written permission.

    In exchange for my granting you this permission, you have agreed to give me _____ free copies of the reproduction, which I may sell or give away as I choose. Those copies will be shipped to my home address by the most efficient carrier.

    Thanks again for your interest. I look forward to working with you on this publication of my work.

Sincerely yours,

_____
_____
_____
_____

ACKNOWLEDGED:

_____ _____
SIGNATURE   DATE

_____
TITLE

Allowing Publication of Reproductions Solely for Promotional Value

_____

_____
_____
_____
_____
_____

Dear _____:

This letter is a follow-up to our recent conversation regarding your interest in publishing a reproduction of my artwork entitled _____ _____. I am very pleased that you want to reproduce my work in this manner, and I only want to clarify a few points regarding this.

   As I explained, my principal concern is the quality of the reproduction. For that reason, I will only grant permission to use my artwork so long as I have the right to approve the selection of printing paper and the proofs of the color separations. Furthermore, while I don't wish to make things difficult for you, I would like to be able to approve the printer's color proofs.

   Under those conditions, I hereby agree to give your company, _____ _____, the right to print _____ copies of my artwork on _____" × _____" sheets. Each of these prints will include my name, the title of the artwork, and the words "Copyright © 19___ by _____." No other use may be made of this or any other of my copyrighted artwork without my written permission.

   In exchange for my granting you this permission, you have agreed to give me _____ free copies of the reproduction, which I may sell or give away as I choose. Those copies will be shipped to my home address by the most efficient carrier.

   Thanks again for your interest. I look forward to working with you on this publication of my work.

                              Sincerely yours,

                              _____
                              _____
                              _____
                              _____

ACKNOWLEDGED:

_____
SIGNATURE   DATE
_____
TITLE

_____

_____
_____
_____
_____
_____

Dear _____:

This letter is a follow-up to our recent conversation regarding your interest in publishing a reproduction of my artwork entitled _____ _____. I am very pleased that you want to reproduce my work in this manner, and I only want to clarify a few points regarding this.

    As I explained, my principal concern is the quality of the reproduction. For that reason, I will only grant permission to use my artwork so long as I have the right to approve the selection of printing paper and the proofs of the color separations. Furthermore, while I don't wish to make things difficult for you, I would like to be able to approve the printer's color proofs.

    Under those conditions, I hereby agree to give your company, _____ _____, the right to print _____ copies of my artwork on _____" × _____" sheets. Each of these prints will include my name, the title of the artwork, and the words "Copyright © 19___ by _____." No other use may be made of this or any other of my copyrighted artwork without my written permission.

    In exchange for my granting you this permission, you have agreed to give me _____ free copies of the reproduction, which I may sell or give away as I choose. Those copies will be shipped to my home address by the most efficient carrier.

    Thanks again for your interest. I look forward to working with you on this publication of my work.

Sincerely yours,

_____
_____
_____
_____

ACKNOWLEDGED:

_____
SIGNATURE   DATE

_____
TITLE

_____

_____
_____
_____
_____
_____

Dear _____:

Thank you for taking the time to discuss the details of our proposed publishing arrangement. It was helpful to review the various aspects of this business proposition, and I believe I have a clear understanding of how we will proceed. I am writing to summarize our agreement, and I would appreciate it if you would sign the enclosed copy of this letter if you agree with all the points covered. If there are any items that need further discussion or revision, please let me know.

First, your company plans to publish reproductions of my artwork, entitled _____, as _____" × _____" prints. There will be an initial printing of _____ copies, with subsequent printings of copies to be discussed, depending on sales. These prints will be distributed through various channels of distribution.

You have agreed that I will have the right to approve the selection of the paper on which the reproductions will be printed, the proofs of the color separations, and proofs from the printer each time that copies are printed. Furthermore, each copy will be printed with my name and a notice of my ownership of the copyright to the image. The notice will read: "Copyright © 19_____ by _____."

I have agreed to accept a _____ percent royalty payment for the sale of each print from the first printing (number). You have indicated this is the standard percentage earned by artists whose works you are currently publishing. I understand that I will receive a _____ statement of sales activity and a check for the amount earned during that period.

In addition, I will receive _____ copies free of charge and will have the option to buy additional copies at _____ for as long as they are in inventory. I may give these away, donate them to nonprofit organizations, or sell them for an amount of money not less than the current wholesale price.

If, at any point, you should want to publish additional copies of this image, I will be happy to discuss that possibility with you and also reevaluate the royalty arrangement. If, on the other hand, you discontinue selling this print, I will have the opportunity to purchase any remaining copies at the manufacturing cost (the price paid for paper, color separations, and printing). These will be mine to use as I please.

I believe that covers all the points we discussed about this publishing project. If you feel we need to have further discussions regarding these or any other matters, please don't hesitate to call or drop me a line. Otherwise, I would appreciate your signing the enclosed copy of this letter and returning it to me at your earliest convenience.

I am eager to see my artwork reproduced as we've discussed and I thank you again for this exciting opportunity.

Sincerely yours,

ACKNOWLEDGED: _____
                                                         _____
_____   _____   _____
SIGNATURE   DATE

_____
TITLE

_____

_____
_____
_____
_____
_____

Dear _____:

Thank you for taking the time to discuss the details of our proposed publishing arrangement. It was helpful to review the various aspects of this business proposition, and I believe I have a clear understanding of how we will proceed. I am writing to summarize our agreement, and I would appreciate it if you would sign the enclosed copy of this letter if you agree with all the points covered. If there are any items that need further discussion or revision, please let me know.

First, your company plans to publish reproductions of my artwork, entitled _____, as _____" × _____" prints. There will be an initial printing of _____ copies, with subsequent printings of copies to be discussed, depending on sales. These prints will be distributed through various channels of distribution.

You have agreed that I will have the right to approve the selection of the paper on which the reproductions will be printed, the proofs of the color separations, and proofs from the printer each time that copies are printed. Furthermore, each copy will be printed with my name and a notice of my ownership of the copyright to the image. The notice will read: "Copyright © 19____ by _____."

I have agreed to accept a _____ percent royalty payment for the sale of each print from the first printing (number). You have indicated this is the standard percentage earned by artists whose works you are currently publishing. I understand that I will receive a _____ statement of sales activity and a check for the amount earned during that period.

In addition, I will receive _____ copies free of charge and will have the option to buy additional copies at _____ for as long as they are in inventory. I may give these away, donate them to nonprofit organizations, or sell them for an amount of money not less than the current wholesale price.

If, at any point, you should want to publish additional copies of this image, I will be happy to discuss that possibility with you and also reevaluate the royalty arrangement. If, on the other hand, you discontinue selling this print, I will have the opportunity to purchase any remaining copies at the manufacturing cost (the price paid for paper, color separations, and printing). These will be mine to use as I please.

I believe that covers all the points we discussed about this publishing project. If you feel we need to have further discussions regarding these or any other matters, please don't hesitate to call or drop me a line. Otherwise, I would appreciate your signing the enclosed copy of this letter and returning it to me at your earliest convenience.

I am eager to see my artwork reproduced as we've discussed and I thank you again for this exciting opportunity.

Sincerely yours,

ACKNOWLEDGED: _____

                                                       _____
_____   _____
SIGNATURE   DATE   _____

_____
TITLE

_____

_____
_____
_____
_____
_____

Dear _____:

Thank you for taking the time to discuss the details of our proposed publishing arrangement. It was helpful to review the various aspects of this business proposition, and I believe I have a clear understanding of how we will proceed. I am writing to summarize our agreement, and I would appreciate it if you would sign the enclosed copy of this letter if you agree with all the points covered. If there are any items that need further discussion or revision, please let me know.

First, your company plans to publish reproductions of my artwork, entitled _____, as _____" × _____" prints. There will be an initial printing of _____ copies, with subsequent printings of copies to be discussed, depending on sales. These prints will be distributed through various channels of distribution.

You have agreed that I will have the right to approve the selection of the paper on which the reproductions will be printed, the proofs of the color separations, and proofs from the printer each time that copies are printed. Furthermore, each copy will be printed with my name and a notice of my ownership of the copyright to the image. The notice will read: "Copyright © 19_____ by _____."

I have agreed to accept a _____ percent royalty payment for the sale of each print from the first printing (number). You have indicated this is the standard percentage earned by artists whose works you are currently publishing. I understand that I will receive a _____ statement of sales activity and a check for the amount earned during that period.

In addition, I will receive _____ copies free of charge and will have the option to buy additional copies at _____ for as long as they are in inventory. I may give these away, donate them to nonprofit organizations, or sell them for an amount of money not less than the current wholesale price.

If, at any point, you should want to publish additional copies of this image, I will be happy to discuss that possibility with you and also reevaluate the royalty arrangement. If, on the other hand, you discontinue selling this print, I will have the opportunity to purchase any remaining copies at the manufacturing cost (the price paid for paper, color separations, and printing). These will be mine to use as I please.

I believe that covers all the points we discussed about this publishing project. If you feel we need to have further discussions regarding these or any other matters, please don't hesitate to call or drop me a line. Otherwise, I would appreciate your signing the enclosed copy of this letter and returning it to me at your earliest convenience.

I am eager to see my artwork reproduced as we've discussed and I thank you again for this exciting opportunity.

Sincerely yours,

ACKNOWLEDGED: _____
                                                _____
_____   _____   _____
SIGNATURE   DATE
_____
TITLE

_____

_____
_____
_____
_____

Dear _____:

This letter sets forth the details of the agreement we discussed during our recent conversation. I would appreciate your reviewing the letter and returning a copy to me with your signature, acknowledging your acceptance of the terms.

    Your company, _____, will produce _____ sculptures/prints/posters/note cards/announcements reproducing my artwork, entitled _____, for a total price of $_____. I enclose a check for $_____, covering the deposit needed/the total amount, with $_____ due upon delivery to me of the finished items in satisfactory condition.

    With this agreement, I grant _____ a limited, nonexclusive license to make reproductions of my artwork solely for sale to me. This license is limited to the specific items and quantities mentioned in this letter and does not extend to any further reproduction of these images.

    You further agree either to destroy or send me any and all proofs which may be made in the production of these items, and you will send me any extra copies that are made. I agree to allow _____ to use some of these items as samples for the promotion of new business.

    Also, _____ agrees to transfer to me all rights to these reproduced items, including the copyright to the images derived from my artwork. Any reproduction of these images in sales literature, company brochures, exhibition catalogs, or other publications must carry a notice stating that I own the copyright.

    I look forward to working with you on this project.

                                 Sincerely yours,

                                 _____
                                 _____
                                 _____
                                 _____

ACKNOWLEDGED:

_____
SIGNATURE   DATE
_____
TITLE

_____

_____
_____
_____
_____

Dear _____:

This letter sets forth the details of the agreement we discussed during our recent conversation. I would appreciate your reviewing the letter and returning a copy to me with your signature, acknowledging your acceptance of the terms.

Your company, _____, will produce _____ sculptures/prints/posters/note cards/announcements reproducing my artwork, entitled _____, for a total price of $_____. I enclose a check for $_____, covering the deposit needed/the total amount, with $_____ due upon delivery to me of the finished items in satisfactory condition.

With this agreement, I grant _____ a limited, nonexclusive license to make reproductions of my artwork solely for sale to me. This license is limited to the specific items and quantities mentioned in this letter and does not extend to any further reproduction of these images.

You further agree either to destroy or send me any and all proofs which may be made in the production of these items, and you will send me any extra copies that are made. I agree to allow _____ to use some of these items as samples for the promotion of new business.

Also, _____ agrees to transfer to me all rights to these reproduced items, including the copyright to the images derived from my artwork. Any reproduction of these images in sales literature, company brochures, exhibition catalogs, or other publications must carry a notice stating that I own the copyright.

I look forward to working with you on this project.

Sincerely yours,

_____
_____
_____
_____

ACKNOWLEDGED:

_____
SIGNATURE   DATE

_____
TITLE

_____   _____

_____

_____

_____

Dear _____:

This letter sets forth the details of the agreement we discussed during our recent conversation. I would appreciate your reviewing the letter and returning a copy to me with your signature, acknowledging your acceptance of the terms.

Your company, _____, will produce _____ sculptures/prints/posters/note cards/announcements reproducing my artwork, entitled _____, for a total price of $_____. I enclose a check for $_____, covering the deposit needed/the total amount, with $_____ due upon delivery to me of the finished items in satisfactory condition.

With this agreement, I grant _____ a limited, nonexclusive license to make reproductions of my artwork solely for sale to me. This license is limited to the specific items and quantities mentioned in this letter and does not extend to any further reproduction of these images.

You further agree either to destroy or send me any and all proofs which may be made in the production of these items, and you will send me any extra copies that are made. I agree to allow _____ to use some of these items as samples for the promotion of new business.

Also, _____ agrees to transfer to me all rights to these reproduced items, including the copyright to the images derived from my artwork. Any reproduction of these images in sales literature, company brochures, exhibition catalogs, or other publications must carry a notice stating that I own the copyright.

I look forward to working with you on this project.

Sincerely yours,

_____

_____

_____

_____

ACKNOWLEDGED:

_____
SIGNATURE   DATE

_____
TITLE

Confirming a Portrait Commission Directly with a Client

_____   _____
_____
_____

Dear _____:

As a follow-up to our recent conversation regarding a portrait of _____
_____, I want briefly to describe some of the arrangements
we have discussed. These will, I hope, set your mind at ease about how I plan to
go about creating this portrait and will clarify the time and financial commitments
I will need from you in order to do the best job possible.

I am quite pleased to have this opportunity. We are furthering a great artistic
tradition, that of creating a portrait through the collaboration of a patron and an
artist. I hope this will prove to be as enjoyable for you as I know it will be for me,
and that this portrait will become something that is treasured for generations.

After years of experience, I have learned that I create my best work when I
follow a schedule of sittings as described on the enclosed sheet. You'll see that I
have outlined the number and duration of the sittings, as well as my need to have
access to articles of clothing, jewelry, etc. Please note that in the course of these
sittings I will produce sketches, studies, and photographs and that I will retain
ownership of these. This schedule is, of course, a general outline, and I will work
out a specific plan that meets both our schedules.

My fee for the portrait, at the size we have discussed, is $_____.
In keeping with standard professional practices, I ask that you give me a deposit of
_____ percent of that amount when we meet for the first sitting. The balance
of the money would be payable when you accept the completed portrait.

People sometimes feel concerned about whether they will be pleased with
the portrait they have commissioned, and I want to assure you that I will make
every reasonable effort to create a work that satisfies you completely. If, in the
end, you are not completely satisfied with the portrait, you will be under no
obligation to accept it or pay the balance of the money. However, the deposit and
the artwork will be mine to keep if you choose not to accept the portrait.

I will give you a call in a few days to answer any questions you may have
about this commission. Once you are comfortable with the arrangements we have
discussed, I would appreciate your sending me the enclosed copy of this letter
with your signature.

I look forward to working with you.

Sincerely yours,

_____
_____
_____
_____

ACKNOWLEDGED:

_____
SIGNATURE   DATE

_____
TITLE

Confirming a Portrait Commission Directly with a Client

_____

_____

_____

_____

Dear _____:

As a follow-up to our recent conversation regarding a portrait of _____
_____, I want briefly to describe some of the arrangements
we have discussed. These will, I hope, set your mind at ease about how I plan to
go about creating this portrait and will clarify the time and financial commitments
I will need from you in order to do the best job possible.

I am quite pleased to have this opportunity. We are furthering a great artistic
tradition, that of creating a portrait through the collaboration of a patron and an
artist. I hope this will prove to be as enjoyable for you as I know it will be for me,
and that this portrait will become something that is treasured for generations.

After years of experience, I have learned that I create my best work when I
follow a schedule of sittings as described on the enclosed sheet. You'll see that I
have outlined the number and duration of the sittings, as well as my need to have
access to articles of clothing, jewelry, etc. Please note that in the course of these
sittings I will produce sketches, studies, and photographs and that I will retain
ownership of these. This schedule is, of course, a general outline, and I will work
out a specific plan that meets both our schedules.

My fee for the portrait, at the size we have discussed, is $_____.
In keeping with standard professional practices, I ask that you give me a deposit of
_____ percent of that amount when we meet for the first sitting. The balance
of the money would be payable when you accept the completed portrait.

People sometimes feel concerned about whether they will be pleased with
the portrait they have commissioned, and I want to assure you that I will make
every reasonable effort to create a work that satisfies you completely. If, in the
end, you are not completely satisfied with the portrait, you will be under no
obligation to accept it or pay the balance of the money. However, the deposit and
the artwork will be mine to keep if you choose not to accept the portrait.

I will give you a call in a few days to answer any questions you may have
about this commission. Once you are comfortable with the arrangements we have
discussed, I would appreciate your sending me the enclosed copy of this letter
with your signature.

I look forward to working with you.

Sincerely yours,

_____

_____

_____

_____

ACKNOWLEDGED:

_____

SIGNATURE   DATE

_____

TITLE

_____   _____
_____
_____

Dear _____:

As a follow-up to our recent conversation regarding a portrait of _____
_____, I want briefly to describe some of the arrangements
we have discussed. These will, I hope, set your mind at ease about how I plan to
go about creating this portrait and will clarify the time and financial commitments
I will need from you in order to do the best job possible.

   I am quite pleased to have this opportunity. We are furthering a great artistic
tradition, that of creating a portrait through the collaboration of a patron and an
artist. I hope this will prove to be as enjoyable for you as I know it will be for me,
and that this portrait will become something that is treasured for generations.

   After years of experience, I have learned that I create my best work when I
follow a schedule of sittings as described on the enclosed sheet. You'll see that I
have outlined the number and duration of the sittings, as well as my need to have
access to articles of clothing, jewelry, etc. Please note that in the course of these
sittings I will produce sketches, studies, and photographs and that I will retain
ownership of these. This schedule is, of course, a general outline, and I will work
out a specific plan that meets both our schedules.

   My fee for the portrait, at the size we have discussed, is $_____.
In keeping with standard professional practices, I ask that you give me a deposit of
_____ percent of that amount when we meet for the first sitting. The balance
of the money would be payable when you accept the completed portrait.

   People sometimes feel concerned about whether they will be pleased with
the portrait they have commissioned, and I want to assure you that I will make
every reasonable effort to create a work that satisfies you completely. If, in the
end, you are not completely satisfied with the portrait, you will be under no
obligation to accept it or pay the balance of the money. However, the deposit and
the artwork will be mine to keep if you choose not to accept the portrait.

   I will give you a call in a few days to answer any questions you may have
about this commission. Once you are comfortable with the arrangements we have
discussed, I would appreciate your sending me the enclosed copy of this letter
with your signature.

   I look forward to working with you.

                                        Sincerely yours,

                                        _____
                                        _____
                                        _____
                                        _____

ACKNOWLEDGED:

_____
SIGNATURE   DATE
_____
TITLE

Establishing a Business Relationship with a Portrait Agent

_____   _____
_____
_____
_____

Dear _____:

I valued our recent conversation about the possibility of having your company represent me as one of its portrait artists. It seems clear that this will work out to be a pleasant and profitable relationship between us. I sincerely appreciate your interest in my work and hope that we'll do a lot of business in the future.

I have been considering the best way for us to work together, while still allowing me to maintain the portrait business I have developed over the years on my own and with other representatives; it made sense to me to write down some of my concerns and needs. If you are in agreement that the points below could be the basis of our working relationship, then I would appreciate your signing a copy of this letter and returning it to me at your earliest convenience. If, on the other hand, you would like to discuss some of these matters further, please let me know.

I mentioned that I have a standard form that I give to clients, which outlines how I go about painting a portrait. I am enclosing a copy of that form so you can see what I need in terms of the number of sessions with the client, how I handle photography, what I expect in terms of travel and accommodations, and so on.

I have always enjoyed working with representatives and have made sure they received their commissions for the work I did for their clients. At the same time, a good portion of the work I do comes to me as a result of my own promotional efforts, or from referrals made by previous clients. Therefore, it should be our understanding that you will receive a commission only on portraits I do (1) for clients you bring to me or (2) for clients obtained as a direct result of recommendations made by people whose commissions you arranged for me. You will not be entitled to a commission on portraits for clients obtained as a result of my own or other agents' promotional efforts.

I think it would be useful to establish a time frame for this agreement and then review our business relationship towards the end of that time. I suggest that the time period be _____ from the date of this letter.

If this letter accurately represents your understanding of our business relationship, I would appreciate your acknowledging that by signing a copy of this letter and returning it to me at your earliest convenience. If, on the other hand, there are matters that need further clarification, please let me know.

I look forward to working with you and your staff and appreciate this opportunity to have my portraits presented to your clients.

Sincerely yours,

ACKNOWLEDGED: _____
                                          _____
_____   _____
SIGNATURE   DATE   _____

TITLE

_____   _____
_____
_____
_____

Dear _____:

I valued our recent conversation about the possibility of having your company represent me as one of its portrait artists. It seems clear that this will work out to be a pleasant and profitable relationship between us. I sincerely appreciate your interest in my work and hope that we'll do a lot of business in the future.

I have been considering the best way for us to work together, while still allowing me to maintain the portrait business I have developed over the years on my own and with other representatives; it made sense to me to write down some of my concerns and needs. If you are in agreement that the points below could be the basis of our working relationship, then I would appreciate your signing a copy of this letter and returning it to me at your earliest convenience. If, on the other hand, you would like to discuss some of these matters further, please let me know.

I mentioned that I have a standard form that I give to clients, which outlines how I go about painting a portrait. I am enclosing a copy of that form so you can see what I need in terms of the number of sessions with the client, how I handle photography, what I expect in terms of travel and accommodations, and so on.

I have always enjoyed working with representatives and have made sure they received their commissions for the work I did for their clients. At the same time, a good portion of the work I do comes to me as a result of my own promotional efforts, or from referrals made by previous clients. Therefore, it should be our understanding that you will receive a commission only on portraits I do (1) for clients you bring to me or (2) for clients obtained as a direct result of recommendations made by people whose commissions you arranged for me. You will not be entitled to a commission on portraits for clients obtained as a result of my own or other agents' promotional efforts.

I think it would be useful to establish a time frame for this agreement and then review our business relationship towards the end of that time. I suggest that the time period be _____ from the date of this letter.

If this letter accurately represents your understanding of our business relationship, I would appreciate your acknowledging that by signing a copy of this letter and returning it to me at your earliest convenience. If, on the other hand, there are matters that need further clarification, please let me know.

I look forward to working with you and your staff and appreciate this opportunity to have my portraits presented to your clients.

Sincerely yours,

ACKNOWLEDGED: _____
                                                   _____
_____ _____   _____
SIGNATURE   DATE

_____
TITLE

Establishing a Business Relationship with a Portrait Agent

_____

_____
_____
_____
_____

Dear _____:

I valued our recent conversation about the possibility of having your company represent me as one of its portrait artists. It seems clear that this will work out to be a pleasant and profitable relationship between us. I sincerely appreciate your interest in my work and hope that we'll do a lot of business in the future.

I have been considering the best way for us to work together, while still allowing me to maintain the portrait business I have developed over the years on my own and with other representatives; it made sense to me to write down some of my concerns and needs. If you are in agreement that the points below could be the basis of our working relationship, then I would appreciate your signing a copy of this letter and returning it to me at your earliest convenience. If, on the other hand, you would like to discuss some of these matters further, please let me know.

I mentioned that I have a standard form that I give to clients, which outlines how I go about painting a portrait. I am enclosing a copy of that form so you can see what I need in terms of the number of sessions with the client, how I handle photography, what I expect in terms of travel and accommodations, and so on.

I have always enjoyed working with representatives and have made sure they received their commissions for the work I did for their clients. At the same time, a good portion of the work I do comes to me as a result of my own promotional efforts, or from referrals made by previous clients. Therefore, it should be our understanding that you will receive a commission only on portraits I do (1) for clients you bring to me or (2) for clients obtained as a direct result of recommendations made by people whose commissions you arranged for me. You will not be entitled to a commission on portraits for clients obtained as a result of my own or other agents' promotional efforts.

I think it would be useful to establish a time frame for this agreement and then review our business relationship towards the end of that time. I suggest that the time period be _____ from the date of this letter.

If this letter accurately represents your understanding of our business relationship, I would appreciate your acknowledging that by signing a copy of this letter and returning it to me at your earliest convenience. If, on the other hand, there are matters that need further clarification, please let me know.

I look forward to working with you and your staff and appreciate this opportunity to have my portraits presented to your clients.

Sincerely yours,

ACKNOWLEDGED: _____
                                                    _____
_____   _____
SIGNATURE   DATE

TITLE

Defining the Stages of a Mural Commission

_____

_____

_____   _____

Dear _____:

I found our recent discussion to be informative and helpful, and I appreciate having gotten more information about the mural you wish to have created for _____ _____. I'm excited about this project and appreciate the opportunity to be part of it.

      Just to be sure we both understand the terms and conditions under which I might be creating this mural, I thought it would be helpful to review the items we covered in our recent discussion. If it occurs to you that I have not covered all the important aspects of this project, or that my recollection of the conversation is not completely accurate, please let me know as soon as possible. If, on the other hand, you feel this letter is an accurate summary of our agreement, I would appreciate your signing a copy and returning it to me.

      You have established that you want a mural on the subject of _____ _____ to be executed in _____ , measuring _____ × _____. It will be attached to a wall in or at _____ _____. The mural must have the following features, details, or motifs: _____
_____
You would like to have the mural completed and installed by _____.

      I have agreed to do a color sketch of my idea(s) so that you have a clear notion of the artwork I propose to create. This sketch will be fairly rough, but will be made to the scale of the finished mural and will be accurate enough to give you a clear idea of the overall composition. I expect to be able to deliver the sketch by _____, at which time we can discuss any changes you think might improve the final artwork.

      It is in our best interest to resolve any potential problems at this stage, and I will be happy to make revisions in the color sketch or to create a new sketch, if that will help us reach agreement about the final appearance of the mural. Because of the time and creative energy involved in developing these sketches, I will consider your initial deposit to be nonrefundable after you approve the color sketch.

      After receiving your approval of the color sketch, I will need _____ months to complete the mural, and I anticipate that I would need _____ days to install the mural.

      The total cost of the mural will be $_____, with a ___ percent deposit of $_____ due with this agreement, and the balance due on completion of the project. This fee will/will not include the expenses for the artwork and for transportation to and installation at the site.

      Any and all drawings, sketches, color studies, or photographs that I use in creating this mural will be mine to keep, and I will retain the copyright to those preparatory works as well as the final image of the mural, unless we negotiate a separate agreement for the transfer of that copyright.

      Again, my thanks to you for giving me the opportunity to work on this exciting project.

Sincerely yours,

ACKNOWLEDGED: _____

_____   _____

SIGNATURE   DATE   _____

TITLE

_____

_____
_____
_____

Dear _____:

I found our recent discussion to be informative and helpful, and I appreciate having gotten more information about the mural you wish to have created for _____ _____. I'm excited about this project and appreciate the opportunity to be part of it.

Just to be sure we both understand the terms and conditions under which I might be creating this mural, I thought it would be helpful to review the items we covered in our recent discussion. If it occurs to you that I have not covered all the important aspects of this project, or that my recollection of the conversation is not completely accurate, please let me know as soon as possible. If, on the other hand, you feel this letter is an accurate summary of our agreement, I would appreciate your signing a copy and returning it to me.

You have established that you want a mural on the subject of _____ _____ to be executed in _____ , measuring _____ × _____. It will be attached to a wall in or at _____ _____. The mural must have the following features, details, or motifs: _____ _____

You would like to have the mural completed and installed by _____.

I have agreed to do a color sketch of my idea(s) so that you have a clear notion of the artwork I propose to create. This sketch will be fairly rough, but will be made to the scale of the finished mural and will be accurate enough to give you a clear idea of the overall composition. I expect to be able to deliver the sketch by _____, at which time we can discuss any changes you think might improve the final artwork.

It is in our best interest to resolve any potential problems at this stage, and I will be happy to make revisions in the color sketch or to create a new sketch, if that will help us reach agreement about the final appearance of the mural. Because of the time and creative energy involved in developing these sketches, I will consider your initial deposit to be nonrefundable after you approve the color sketch.

After receiving your approval of the color sketch, I will need ____ months to complete the mural, and I anticipate that I would need _____ days to install the mural.

The total cost of the mural will be $_____, with a ___ percent deposit of $_____ due with this agreement, and the balance due on completion of the project. This fee will/will not include the expenses for the artwork and for transportation to and installation at the site.

Any and all drawings, sketches, color studies, or photographs that I use in creating this mural will be mine to keep, and I will retain the copyright to those preparatory works as well as the final image of the mural, unless we negotiate a separate agreement for the transfer of that copyright.

Again, my thanks to you for giving me the opportunity to work on this exciting project.

Sincerely yours,

_____
_____
ACKNOWLEDGED: _____
                                                 _____
_____ _____
SIGNATURE   DATE

_____
TITLE

Defining the Stages of a Mural Commission

Dear _____:

I found our recent discussion to be informative and helpful, and I appreciate having gotten more information about the mural you wish to have created for _____ _____. I'm excited about this project and appreciate the opportunity to be part of it.

Just to be sure we both understand the terms and conditions under which I might be creating this mural, I thought it would be helpful to review the items we covered in our recent discussion. If it occurs to you that I have not covered all the important aspects of this project, or that my recollection of the conversation is not completely accurate, please let me know as soon as possible. If, on the other hand, you feel this letter is an accurate summary of our agreement, I would appreciate your signing a copy and returning it to me.

You have established that you want a mural on the subject of _____ _____ to be executed in _____ , measuring _____ × _____. It will be attached to a wall in or at _____ _____. The mural must have the following features, details, or motifs: _____ _____

You would like to have the mural completed and installed by _____.

I have agreed to do a color sketch of my idea(s) so that you have a clear notion of the artwork I propose to create. This sketch will be fairly rough, but will be made to the scale of the finished mural and will be accurate enough to give you a clear idea of the overall composition. I expect to be able to deliver the sketch by _____, at which time we can discuss any changes you think might improve the final artwork.

It is in our best interest to resolve any potential problems at this stage, and I will be happy to make revisions in the color sketch or to create a new sketch, if that will help us reach agreement about the final appearance of the mural. Because of the time and creative energy involved in developing these sketches, I will consider your initial deposit to be nonrefundable after you approve the color sketch.

After receiving your approval of the color sketch, I will need ____ months to complete the mural, and I anticipate that I would need _____ days to install the mural.

The total cost of the mural will be $_____, with a ___ percent deposit of $_____ due with this agreement, and the balance due on completion of the project. This fee will/will not include the expenses for the artwork and for transportation to and installation at the site.

Any and all drawings, sketches, color studies, or photographs that I use in creating this mural will be mine to keep, and I will retain the copyright to those preparatory works as well as the final image of the mural, unless we negotiate a separate agreement for the transfer of that copyright.

Again, my thanks to you for giving me the opportunity to work on this exciting project.

Sincerely yours,

ACKNOWLEDGED:

_____
SIGNATURE   DATE

_____
TITLE

Establishing a Commission to Create Artwork

_____

_____
_____
_____

Dear _____ :

Concerning our recent conversation about the possibility of creating a work of art for you, I am certainly pleased by your interest in such a project. In order to go further with this idea, it would be helpful to me to state here what you have requested, the time frame for this commission, and the financial terms that we might agree to.

You have indicated you would like to have a _____ work on the subject of _____ for display in or at your _____ _____. It will have the following specific features: _____ _____

The completed artwork would measure _____ × _____ and would be displayed by _____ , 19____.

In a situation like this, it is common practice for an artist to prepare a color sketch of an idea for a commissioned work and then have the client either approve the sketch or suggest changes. I propose to make a rough color sketch of my design, in scale with the size of the final work. Though the sketch would not be as detailed or refined as the final artwork, it would be clear enough to indicate the overall composition.

Because I want you to be satisfied with the artwork you commission, I will be happy to discuss changes in the color sketch and, if necessary, will create revised sketches. If, after reviewing these various sketches you are not completely satisfied, you can cancel the project without any obligation. On the other hand, if you approve a final color sketch and want me to proceed, then to begin working I will need a nonrefundable deposit of _____ percent of the total price of the work.

The total price of the commission will be $_____. Assuming you do approve the color sketch and give me a deposit, then the balance would be due on delivery. I anticipate that it would take me approximately _____ weeks/months to complete the work after you approve the color sketch.

I look forward to this project, and I'm eager to begin work on the sketch. I do wish to make sure I have clearly stated your ideas on the commission and would like to get your response to this letter. If you have any further thoughts about the artwork, please let me know. If what I have described here seems accurate, and you are in agreement about the terms of the commission, then I would appreciate your signing the enclosed copy of the letter and returning it to me at your earliest convenience.

Sincerely yours,

ACKNOWLEDGED: _____
                                                _____
_____   _____
SIGNATURE   DATE   _____
_____
TITLE

_____

_____
_____
_____

Dear _____:

Concerning our recent conversation about the possibility of creating a work of art for you, I am certainly pleased by your interest in such a project. In order to go further with this idea, it would be helpful to me to state here what you have requested, the time frame for this commission, and the financial terms that we might agree to.

You have indicated you would like to have a _____ work on the subject of _____ for display in or at your _____ _____. It will have the following specific features: _____

_____
The completed artwork would measure _____ × _____ and would be displayed by _____ , 19____.

In a situation like this, it is common practice for an artist to prepare a color sketch of an idea for a commissioned work and then have the client either approve the sketch or suggest changes. I propose to make a rough color sketch of my design, in scale with the size of the final work. Though the sketch would not be as detailed or refined as the final artwork, it would be clear enough to indicate the overall composition.

Because I want you to be satisfied with the artwork you commission, I will be happy to discuss changes in the color sketch and, if necessary, will create revised sketches. If, after reviewing these various sketches you are not completely satisfied, you can cancel the project without any obligation. On the other hand, if you approve a final color sketch and want me to proceed, then to begin working I will need a nonrefundable deposit of _____ percent of the total price of the work.

The total price of the commission will be $_____. Assuming you do approve the color sketch and give me a deposit, then the balance would be due on delivery. I anticipate that it would take me approximately _____ weeks/months to complete the work after you approve the color sketch.

I look forward to this project, and I'm eager to begin work on the sketch. I do wish to make sure I have clearly stated your ideas on the commission and would like to get your response to this letter. If you have any further thoughts about the artwork, please let me know. If what I have described here seems accurate, and you are in agreement about the terms of the commission, then I would appreciate your signing the enclosed copy of the letter and returning it to me at your earliest convenience.

Sincerely yours,

ACKNOWLEDGED: _____
                                        _____
_____   _____
SIGNATURE   DATE   _____

TITLE

Establishing a Commission to Create Artwork

_____
_____
_____

_____

Dear _____:

Concerning our recent conversation about the possibility of creating a work of art for you, I am certainly pleased by your interest in such a project. In order to go further with this idea, it would be helpful to me to state here what you have requested, the time frame for this commission, and the financial terms that we might agree to.

You have indicated you would like to have a _____ work on the subject of _____ for display in or at your _____ _____. It will have the following specific features: _____ _____
The completed artwork would measure _____ × _____ and would be displayed by _____ , 19____.

In a situation like this, it is common practice for an artist to prepare a color sketch of an idea for a commissioned work and then have the client either approve the sketch or suggest changes. I propose to make a rough color sketch of my design, in scale with the size of the final work. Though the sketch would not be as detailed or refined as the final artwork, it would be clear enough to indicate the overall composition.

Because I want you to be satisfied with the artwork you commission, I will be happy to discuss changes in the color sketch and, if necessary, will create revised sketches. If, after reviewing these various sketches you are not completely satisfied, you can cancel the project without any obligation. On the other hand, if you approve a final color sketch and want me to proceed, then to begin working I will need a nonrefundable deposit of _____ percent of the total price of the work.

The total price of the commission will be $_____. Assuming you do approve the color sketch and give me a deposit, then the balance would be due on delivery. I anticipate that it would take me approximately _____ weeks/months to complete the work after you approve the color sketch.

I look forward to this project, and I'm eager to begin work on the sketch. I do wish to make sure I have clearly stated your ideas on the commission and would like to get your response to this letter. If you have any further thoughts about the artwork, please let me know. If what I have described here seems accurate, and you are in agreement about the terms of the commission, then I would appreciate your signing the enclosed copy of the letter and returning it to me at your earliest convenience.

Sincerely yours,

ACKNOWLEDGED: _____
                                        _____
_____   _____
SIGNATURE   DATE

_____
TITLE

_____   _____

_____

_____

_____

Dear _____:

Concerning our recent conversation about the possibility of creating a work of art for you, I am certainly pleased by your interest in such a project. In order to go further with this idea, it would be helpful to me to state here what you have requested, the time frame for this commission, and the financial terms that we might agree to.

You have indicated you would like to have a _____ work on the subject of _____ for display in or at your _____ _____. It will have the following specific features: _____ _____

The completed artwork would measure _____ × _____ and would be displayed by _____ , 19____.

In a situation like this, it is common practice for an artist to prepare a color sketch of an idea for a commissioned work and then have the client either approve the sketch or suggest changes. I propose to make a rough color sketch of my design, in scale with the size of the final work. Though the sketch would not be as detailed or refined as the final artwork, it would be clear enough to indicate the overall composition.

Because I want you to be satisfied with the artwork you commission, I will be happy to discuss changes in the color sketch and, if necessary, will create revised sketches. If, after reviewing these various sketches you are not completely satisfied, you can cancel the project without any obligation. On the other hand, if you approve a final color sketch and want me to proceed, then to begin working I will need a nonrefundable deposit of _____ percent of the total price of the work.

The total price of the commission will be $_____. Assuming you do approve the color sketch and give me a deposit, then the balance would be due on delivery. I anticipate that it would take me approximately _____ weeks/months to complete the work after you approve the color sketch.

I look forward to this project, and I'm eager to begin work on the sketch. I do wish to make sure I have clearly stated your ideas on the commission and would like to get your response to this letter. If you have any further thoughts about the artwork, please let me know. If what I have described here seems accurate, and you are in agreement about the terms of the commission, then I would appreciate your signing the enclosed copy of the letter and returning it to me at your earliest convenience.

Sincerely yours,

ACKNOWLEDGED: _____

_____   _____

SIGNATURE   DATE   _____

TITLE

_____

MODEL RELEASE

I hereby agree to pose as a model for _____ for a
fee of $_____ per hour. I grant him/her permission to draw, paint, or otherwise record
my image in any form or medium and to take photographs of me for the purposes of
creating these works of art. Furthermore, I grant him/her permission to exhibit, publish,
and or sell these works without any claims being made by me.

   I hereby warrant that I am of legal age, have the right to establish this agreement
in my own name, and that these permissions are granted to _____, successors, legal representative, and assigns. Further, I warrant that I have read this model
release agreement and agree to its contents.

_____   _____   _____   _____
SIGNATURE   DATE   WITNESS   DATE

_____   _____
ADDRESS   ADDRESS

_____

MODEL RELEASE

I hereby agree to pose as a model for _____ for a fee of $_____ per hour. I grant him/her permission to draw, paint, or otherwise record my image in any form or medium and to take photographs of me for the purposes of creating these works of art. Furthermore, I grant him/her permission to exhibit, publish, and or sell these works without any claims being made by me.

I hereby warrant that I am of legal age, have the right to establish this agreement in my own name, and that these permissions are granted to _____, successors, legal representative, and assigns. Further, I warrant that I have read this model release agreement and agree to its contents.

_____ _____   _____ _____
SIGNATURE   DATE   WITNESS   DATE

_____   _____
ADDRESS   ADDRESS

_____

MODEL RELEASE

I hereby agree to pose as a model for _____ for a fee of $_____ per hour. I grant him/her permission to draw, paint, or otherwise record my image in any form or medium and to take photographs of me for the purposes of creating these works of art. Furthermore, I grant him/her permission to exhibit, publish, and or sell these works without any claims being made by me.

    I hereby warrant that I am of legal age, have the right to establish this agreement in my own name, and that these permissions are granted to _____, successors, legal representative, and assigns. Further, I warrant that I have read this model release agreement and agree to its contents.

_____   _____   _____   _____

SIGNATURE   DATE   WITNESS   DATE

_____   _____

ADDRESS   ADDRESS

Dear _____ :

DESCRIPTION:

AMOUNT DUE $_____._____

Thank you,

Dear _____:

DESCRIPTION:

AMOUNT DUE $_____._____

Thank you,